The Aesthetic
Townscape

The MIT Press   *Cambridge,*   *London, England*
Massachusetts

basis and his designing and building on a full-time basis.

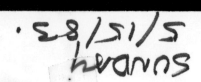

The Aesthetic Townscape by Yoshinobu Ashihara (MIT; $20) is a well-designed collection of observations on how people perceive space and how that perception shapes cities. One of Japan's most distinguished architects,

Ashihara explores the impact of a variety of spatial concepts, building designs and streetscapes in both the East and the West, with a particular emphasis on scenes in his native land and Italy. The style is engagingly direct for a subject that in the past has been burdened by architects trying to make a science out of their observations. Though a summary would have been helpful, there are enough insights throughout to make the whole a practical aid for planners, architects and, indeed, anyone who appreciates cities.

"Yoshinobu Ashihara, one of Japan's most distinguished architects, and teacher of architecture and planning, has written a wonderful …

$20.00

This book was set in Baskerville by The MIT
Press Computergraphics Department and
printed and bound by Halliday Lithograph in
the United States of America.

Library of Congress Cataloging in
Publication Data

Ashihara, Yoshinobu, 1918–
The aesthetic townscape.
Translation of: Machinami no bigaku.
Bibliography: p.
Includes index.
1. Space (Architecture) 2. City planning.
3. Architectural design. I. Title.
NA9053.S6A8313 1983   729   82-17244
ISBN 0-262-01069-0

Contents

Acknowledgments

The publication of this book on the aesthetics of the townscape realizes a long-envisioned dream. In the course of traveling around the world observing the architecture and townscapes of different countries and regions, it occurred to me that it might be valuable to put together a volume recording my studies and impressions of these townscapes. One important reason for doing this is that I believe treatment of space in Japan is different from other cultures. I believe that in the comparative study of culture Japan's unique approach to space, to this day a determining characteristic of its architecture, is useful to both westerners and Japanese in explaining western concepts of space.

I am indebted to many people for making the publication of this book possible. Foremost are my old friend Nathan Glazer, who was also instrumental in the publication of my earlier book, *Exterior Design in Architecture*, for his encouragement and sound advice on the original draft translation of this work, and my respected friend Kevin Lynch for his reading of the manuscript and valuable comments.

This book is based on my work in Japanese, *Machinami no bigaku* ("The Aesthetics of the Townscape") published by Iwanami Shoten in 1979. In consideration of the interests of readers of the English edition, however, major portions have been rewritten and new material added. The photographs are in large part my own, but I include many fine ones by Yukio Futagawa and other professional photographers. I am particularly fortunate to have had the contributions of talented illustrator Hiroshi Ohba and also of Gakutoshi Kojima of my staff.

I would like to express sincerest thanks to Lynne E. Riggs for her sensitive and careful translation of the original Japanese text and subsequent revised portions over two years in the preparation of this work for publication in English, and to my secretaries Yūko Sakuma and Naomi Masuda for their devoted efforts and assistance. Publication of this book in the United States, moreover, would not have been possible without the generosity and cooperation of the staff of the MIT Press and Kōshi Takeda of Iwanami Shoten.

Introduction

After observing architecture and cities around the world, I am convinced that the key explanation for the great diversity in basic perceptions of space lies in the nature of the boundary that distinguishes internal from external space and in the treatment of territorial space. A townscape is born of the relationship between man and his culture and a particular natural environment; it is a manifestation of a community's temporal and spatial conception of its existence. Trying to change the fundamental character of a townscape is thus as difficult as attempting to alter the entire climate and culture of the locality. The difficulties have been amply demonstrated in the efforts to build planned cities like Brasilia and Chandigarh. Yet, for the benefit of people who must live in the cities, it is urgent that we design and build more attractive residential environments and townscapes. We need not go so far as to design completely new cities or vast projects of urban renewal; we must simply try to understand a city as it is, preserving its good attributes and replacing its bad, and devise townscapes that are at least a little more beautiful, pleasant, and memorable. One way we can begin is by comparing the townscapes of countries in various climates and by gaining a genuine appreciation of their unique character, as I have in this book.

It is important to examine what a given people think of as internal space and where external space begins, as well as what they think of as external space and where internal space begins; we also need a better perception of how the boundary line between inside and outside is established. Japanese customarily observe an explicit distinction between "inside" and "outside" space within the townscape. By contrast, I believe that the architecture of the West demonstrates no such distinction between interior and exterior space. Internal and external space is conceived of as equivalent, and this approach, we may note, has been much more conducive to the development of an aesthetically pleasing townscape and a sense of community.

Plans that opt to unite space from outside to inside—the orthodox method of city planning—involve traffic systems, land use, and long-term urban development. This approach is typically western, however, and suffers from a lack of sensitivity to the voices of city residents, giving them little sense of participation. This very predicament has brought city planning to an impasse in recent years.

Japanese habitually shun long-term and large-scale planning; things tend to develop spontaneously, in the on-going course of events. This is reflected in Japanese cities today, and they are widely criticized for lack of planning and absence of distinctive character. Nevertheless, in their own fashion, Japanese cities have a quite democratic, human dimension that cannot altogether be discounted. Though they may appear at first glance unplanned and disorderly, Japanese cities embrace many parts, each with its own internal order, and it is the collective character of these parts that distinguishes the Japanese urban scene from its counterpart in the West.

An alternative to western city planning, I might suggest then, would begin with internal space. In planning space, one might be able to "internalize" external space rather than "externalize" internal space in the western sense. Accordingly, if one thinks of one's own house as "interior" space, the street outside is "exterior." Then, if one expands the spatial territory somewhat, one may come to think of the street in front, that area most closely associated with his house, as "internalized" inside space. Further expanding the area, one can think of the entire block or immediate community as "inside" or internalized space. The territory can be infinitely expanded, but the most important consideration is the extent to which such "internalization" is possible in a given context. There are naturally limits, and these limits can be thought of as determining the appropriate scale of a townscape.

This book consists of studies I have pursued and written about over thirty years; it is a record of my own personal encounter with and study of the townscape. Naturally, my approach to the western townscape and perception of space is influenced by my Japanese viewpoint. I look forward now to hearing ideas and analyses on Japanese concepts of space from a western standpoint.

The Aesthetic
Townscape

1

*Territories of
Architectural
Space*

Wall versus Floor

Architecture basically refers to structures that have internal space separated from nature by walls or roofs. Such structures as power-line towers or monumental statues, no matter how tall or massive they may be, are categorically excluded. Internal space creates an "inside" function that shelters man against the elements and protects him from the incursions or threats of his enemies. In the small towns of Gaudix and Purullena in southern Spain, people still live in caves dug into the sides of the hills. Inside, these cave dwellings look somewhat like the interiors of buildings of masonry construction, although the exteriors, which are simply the hillsides dotted with white facades and chimneys, hardly seem to resemble what we would call architecture. Still, insofar as they have internal space, they do qualify for the term.

Architectural space can be defined as an area physically demarcated by three boundary elements: a floor, a wall, and a ceiling (figure 1). Internal space is carved out of nature by the tangible presence of these three elements. In this way they establish a spatial order of internal and external. Architecture is what we experience as "inside" as opposed to "outside." By definition, boundaries impose limits on architectural space—a structure of infinite size is inconceivable. Boundaries create spatial order and ultimately determine the quality of the very space they define.

In considering architectural space, we may identify two types of ordering systems: one that is characterized by the wall and another by the floor. First let us consider that in which the wall is the most important boundary element.

A wall is much more than a plane that obstructs a view; by its nature it is responsible for the quality of interior space.

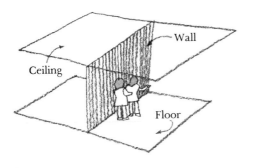

1
Elements of architectural
space

The thickness of a wall is determined not only by considerations of strength, thermal conduction, and sound insulation but also by the quality of internal space desired. In this sense walls are a determining factor of the human condition, a condition that varies from culture to culture.

The walls of Japanese houses, for example, are quite thin. An anecdote about a carpenter who moved into a row house (*nagaya*) in a crowded urban area humorously captures the significance of this. As he drove a nail into his wall one day to hang a picture, he was aghast to find that it had gone clear through the wall and into his neighbor's household altar! Although slightly hyperbolic, as is typical of the tradition of *rakugo* storytelling humor, such an incident would not be altogether impossible; a westerner, whose image of a wall is rather different, perhaps has visions of a nail several inches long.

On the other side of the coin, there is the story told by French writer Marcel Aymé of the civil servant who possessed the power to pass through walls. One day he became so exasperated with the persistent nagging of his supervisor that he placed himself in the wall of the supervisor's office, leaving only his head sticking out.[1] Now it is the Japanese turn to be puzzled. Even if one could accept the idea of the power to go through walls, for them a wall is far too thin—a man could never pass into one. Aymé's story is actually concerned with other things, but it does provide a vivid illustration of the tradition of thick walls in ordinary European buildings. A study some years ago found that the dividing walls of duplexes or row houses in the suburbs of London are on average 70 centimeters thick. It observed that the standard exterior wall of homes in Germany is about 49 centimeters thick, while interior walls are approximately 24 centimeters, meaning that the walls of houses in these areas occupy about 20 percent of the entire floor area.[2] The figures speak eloquently of the importance of walls in European homes.

Walls that set internal space apart from the outside are of particular importance, and in Europe stout and sturdy walls that provide protection are the foremost attribute of an acceptable house. Otto F. Bollnow asserts that in a chaotic, menacing environment man needs above all a firmly established home of his own. He quotes from Antoine de Saint-Exupéry in *Citadelle*, who writes that only with such a "citadel" can man successfully resist the recurrent assaults of the outside world. Saint-Exupéry maintains that man has lost the secure fortifications of the self, without which the ego cannot sustain itself. This citadel must be regained, for only from within such a solid bulwark or enclosure is man able to prevent uncircumscribed forces from invading his territory.[3] Bollnow stresses the importance of a sturdy circumscribing boundary—the wall—and repeatedly emphasizes that only through a "dwelling" place does a man assert his identity. He is by nature "one who dwells," or more precisely, one who adjusts himself to being settled in a given place by contriving walls to defend and protect his territory from alien forces. Bollnow says that, set adrift in the world, man achieves true existence only by possessing space—the space to carry on his activities of living in the broadest sense of the term—not merely by being in space.[4]

In another example of the western concept of a dwelling as shelter against the elements, the French philosopher Gaston Bachelard describes a house struggling, just as would a human being, against a storm, and by its courageous battle, affirming its existence:

The house was fighting gallantly. At first it gave voice to its complaints; the most awful gusts were attacking it from every side at once, with evident hatred and such howls of rage that, at times, I trembled with fear. But it stood firm . . . and stood up to the beast. . . . the house clung close to me, like a she-wolf, and at times, I could smell her odor penetrating maternally to my very heart. That night she was really my mother.[5]

For Japanese, who have lived for centuries in frail-walled dwellings of wood, bamboo, and paper, the existential concept of a house as a place of security and protection has a strange ring. It points to the independence of the individual as the basis of the human condition. In this and many other ways the nature of man's dwelling places ultimately shapes his mode of existence.

The major difference in images of a house in Japan and in Europe is in perceptions of the wall as boundary. Thick, solid walls conjure up an image of interior warmth and comfort against cold, wintery winds. This is the common image in the West.

In Japan a wall enters the consciousness in a quite different way. It is thin, often temporary, and more or less symbolic as a separation of inside and outside. Why does the wall present such an unsubstantial image in the Japanese consciousness? The first reason we may deduce is the sense of continuity with nature that pervades Japanese culture. Rather than erect walls that deliberately cut off nature to create interior space, Japanese feel close to nature and build in a fashion that is open to the out-of-doors. The traditional norm is reflected in *Essays in Idleness* (*Tsurezuregusa*), a classic familiar to all Japanese, by the priest Kenkō (1283–1350): "There is charm about a neat and proper dwelling house, although this world, 'tis true, is but a temporary abode.'"[6] Kenkō states that a house should be built for summer, well ventilated by north–south breezes. The tradition that a house should be an extension of its environment has persisted, and the ideal abode is associated above all with the blossoms of spring, the evening cool of summer, the bright moonlight of autumn, and the hushed snowfall of winter. Perhaps because of this sense of continuity with nature, the tangible aspect of a wall does not stand foremost in the Japanese consciousness of architectural space.

In demarcating space, the role of the wall is primarily symbolic; even if it is imaginary or metaphysical, and even if it does not provide the protection of a real shelter, it is still viable as a wall. In the rituals of the Shintō religion, for example, a sacred area is marked out by setting up four bamboo poles and stretching a twisted rice straw cord called a *shimenawa* with dangling paper symbols between them. White sand is sometimes spread over this area. The *shimenawa* creates a symbolic boundary between inside and outside and marks it as a consecrated space. Although no tangible wall exists, there is an understood and clear distinction between inside and outside (see figure 2). In the construction of the most modern buildings Japanese still continue the time-honored Shintō rituals for ground breaking, raising the "ridge pole," and completion of construction. At each of these ceremonies a consecrated territory delineated by a *shimenawa* is set aside in which rites evoking the gods and ritual purification of the site are conducted.

Another example of such symbolic space is found in customs associated with flower viewing during the cherry blossom season. Traditionally, revelers lay down a

2
Ritual enclosure

red mat beneath the blossoming trees, and friends or family gather upon it to eat, drink, and make merry. The mat clearly demarcates space, uniting those upon it and signaling to outsiders that it is a group (figure 3). Symbolic space is also created by cotton curtains, broadly striped in red and white for auspicious occasions and in black and white for funerals. In these cases the boundary that plays the role of wall is often invisible, or even if visible, it is lightweight, inconspicuous, and temporary. When the space thus created is no longer needed, the accoutrements that mark it can be taken down, and the area will disappear as quickly as it was created, leaving the original landscape unchanged.

One of the best known examples in Japan of such temporary space is to be found in Kyoto. There, during the summer season only, temporary restaurants are created along the Kibune River by building platforms in the river stream where food and drink are served in a pleasant traditional setting. When summer is over, these platform restaurants are taken away, and the river landscape returns to its original state (figures 4 and 5).

In a way the same principle of symbolic, temporary space applies to Japan's tradition of wooden residential architecture. A sense of fluid space is made possible by construction with posts and beams, leaving buildings open, liberated from the confining domination of solid walls. Floors are raised some distance off the ground and trimly laid with clean *tatami* mats made of bundled rice straw. New *tatami* are naturally considered the ideal, for their freshness is considered symbolic of the "sacred space" of a home. Shoes are removed at the entryway, leaving behind the "dust" of the world outside, literally and figuratively.

3
Cherry blossom viewing

4
Restaurant on the
Kibune River in Kyoto
(Photograph: Nobuhiro
Suzuki)

5
Close-up of Kibune
River restaurant
(Photograph: Yoshinobu
Ashihara)

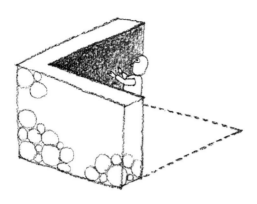

6
Architecture of the wall

With the wall as its dominant feature western masonry architecture can be existentially abstracted as an "architecture of the wall" (figures 6 and 7). In the wooden residential architecture of Japan, the wall figures much less prominently; traditional design ought, by contrast, to be called the "architecture of the floor." It can be symbolized by immaculate, freshly laid *tatami* mats (figures 8 and 9). The background of this rather different attitude toward space derives partly from climate: in Japan's hot, humid summers it was far more important to have good ventilation than solid sheltering walls, and the feeling of closeness rather than resistance to nature makes walls of secondary importance. But perhaps even more significant is the pervasive belief, widespread even today, in the transience of all things—the Buddhist teaching that nothing is permanent.

The basic teachings of Buddhism are that phenomenal things have no substance but are in existence only by condition (*shohō muga*) and that all things are impermanent (*shogyō mujō*), that nothing is fixed but is in constant motion. Life is illusory, and things do not have weight. They are sustained only by their interrelationships. The concept of *muga* or absence of substance is often likened to the flame of a candle, never the same in form or substance from one moment to the next. Man, too, is never the same one day that he was the day before, underlining the importance of the concept of impermanence—*mujō*. In this sense *muga* symbolizes space, and *mujō* represents time; change is constant in both time and space.[7]

This conceptual framework is basic to the distinctive Japanese perception of space. Space is not conceived of as something defined by the heavy material and existential presence of surrounding walls;

7
Italian masonry
construction
(Photograph: Yukio
Futagawa)

8
Architecture of the floor

it is the scene of fluid change and constant transformation, symbolic of the relationship between man and his natural environment.

Naturally, the character of man's shelter is largely determined by local climate, as well as by available materials and methods of construction. In the building of a house, external factors such as rainfall, snowfall, wind velocity, sunlight, and seismic activity are important considerations; yet geographical distribution shows that, throughout time, temperature and especially humidity are controlling factors. Both Japan and Europe, except for parts of southern Europe, belong to the humid zone, and they are richly endowed with forests that provide timber for wood construction. Still, despite this similarity in climate, the European region, except some northern areas, is dominated by urban dwellings of stone and brick masonry contruction, while in Japan wooden post-and-beam construction is most common. The difference in construction methods has had a profound impact on life-styles, as well as on the urban scene and on patterns of city growth. The huge megalopolises of Japan, for example, may appear quite modern at first glance, but they in fact remain under the influence of traditional attitudes that originate in design methods intended for wood construction.

Japan's plentiful rainfall provides an ideal climate for evergreen conifers. Native Japanese varieties of cedar and cypress, which are particularly beautiful as well as durable and easy to work with, are the most common materials for both structural and interior woodwork. One distinctive feature of Japanese architecture is the use of cedar cut on the straight grain or high-quality cypress posts which are deliberately left exposed outside the walls (figure 10). This technique not only

9
Japanese wood
construction as seen in
the Katsura Detached
Palace, Kyoto
(Photograph: Yukio
Futagawa)

10
Structural members
exposed in post-and-
beam construction

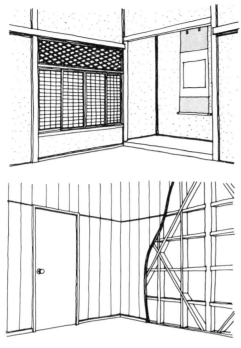

11
Structural members
hidden in stud-wall
construction

demonstrates the skill of the master carpenter but allows the beauty and quality of the woodwork to show in the finished structure. The stud-wall construction common in the West, in which wood is used only for structural members and ultimately hidden completely within the walls, did not develop in Japan (figure 11).

In Japanese residential architecture the standard beam is 10 to 12 centimeters square, a size most convenient in terms of strength, ease of milling, and transport. In a Japanese room built by the post-and-beam construction method, the door and windowsills and the lintels and cross beams are all measured to fall within the posts. Only the exposed tie beams (nage-shi) and ceiling ledges protrude. In the stud-wall construction method, since the beams are merely structural members, the walls can be built as thick as desired. But in a Japanese house in order to allow the natural beauty of these structural elements to show, the walls can be no more than about 10 centimeters thick. The post-and-beam construction method requires that beams be spaced according to a fixed standard, resulting in regular bays between the posts. These bays form a spatial structure that somehow disclaims the existence of walls. The same qualities can also be achieved in a steel frame building, such as Philip Johnson's glass house, a representative work of one period in the development of postwar American architecture.

In a post-and-beam constructed house the door and window frames all fit between the posts, and the shōji (a wooden frame covered with translucent white paper, usually installed in window or door openings) and fusuma (a sliding interior dividing door made of a light wood frame covered with heavy paper) panels used to close off the spaces are approximately 3 centimeters thick. The smooth sliding of these panels is the real test of a well-constructed building; a light *fusuma* panel that slides away smoothly at the touch of a single finger is a wholly different concept in partitioning from the sturdy, thick doors that swing heavily open or closed for each room in a western-style building.

In Japan's climate, where the summers are hot and humid, an airspace below the floor is an important architectural element, and post-and-beam construction is best suited to this need. If a stone or brick masonry structure were raised off the ground on posts, the weight of the building could not be supported, and it would soon collapse. In order to endure hot, humid summers in the age before air-conditioning, natural ventilation was a primary concern, and the openness of post-and-beam construction made such houses particularly well suited to summer living.

Spring and autumn are very pleasant in Japan, but what of the winters? Compared to the superior thermal capacity of a stone or brick house, the thin-walled Japanese-style house with its open construction has little insulation, and the cold of outdoors passes directly inside. Trying to warm the entire inside of such a traditional house is impossible, as hopeless as heating the out-of-doors. Experience has taught residents that it is wisest to use heating methods involving direct contact such as the *hibachi* or charcoal brazier; the *irori* or fireplace in the center of the floor; or the *kotatsu*, a foot-warmer placed under a low table covered with a quilt. These methods of warming the hands and feet are supplemented by food and drink that warm from within, such as hot boiled rice, bubbling thick *miso* soup, or warmed saké, and by thick, padded clothing to keep internal warmth from escaping. A

Japanese house with construction so open and uninsulated simply cannot maintain a constant temperature, so the notion of warming entire rooms did not emerge. Without the thick walls, small windows, and high thermal capacity of masonry structure, it was not practical. The Japanese way of life is fundamentally close to and responsive to nature, and the tradition of cultivating the richest possible lifestyle from the least amount of energy is a long one. In many respects it anticipates the needs of our modern age of energy conservation.

Wooden post-and-beam contruction is a raised type of architecture with an airspace below the floor and, as I have said, has very low heat retention. *Tatami* floors, which are low temperature conducting, encourage the custom of taking off shoes indoors, and sitting or sleeping on mats laid directly on the floor. In masonry houses of western Europe floored with temperature-conducting stone slabs, it is necessary to keep off of the surface, so people keep their shoes on and, quite naturally, find it more comfortable to sleep in beds raised above the floor. In addition Japanese *tatami* absorb the moisture that gathers under bedding during the night. On the stone floors in western houses a bed raised on legs is preferable in this regard, for stone does not absorb moisture.

The masonry wall is, of course, solid; its density begrudges any interruption of pure form. In the simplest architecture, when openings were made, they were often in the form of several long, narrow windows designed in such a way as to assure that the wall's original integrity was in no way impaired. Creating apertures such as doors or windows in masonry walls required special techniques, for they had to be torn, so to speak, out of the solidity and thickness of the structure.

In post-and-beam construction, by contrast, the entire structural area, save for the posts themselves, is potential window or door space. The amount of shelter provided depends on the extent to which these spaces are filled in with walls. The relationship between walls and openings in post-and-beam construction is thus the exact opposite of that in masonry architecture. Here the openings dominate the entire spatial structure, the posts and beams simply providing a supportive role.

A stone or brick wall is not only thick but heavy. Obviously a house with such walls and with small windows imparts to its residents a real feeling of protection. Why, then, did masonry architecture not develop in Japan? As I suggested earlier, there seem to be philosophical reasons for Japanese preferences in building techniques, but considerations of humidity, rainfall, earthquake frequency, and availability of materials are clearly fundamental. The humidity in Japan, particularly in summer, is an important factor. The regions where masonry architecture flourish have dry summers, unlike Japan and Southeast Asia. This suggests that dry summers are a determining factor in the development of masonry construction. In the cave dwellings of Gaudix in Spain, modern residents still enjoy a dry coolness that makes it possible to completely forget the fierce heat of the summer. Cross ventilation in these dwellings is undesirable, for it only introduces hot air from outside, destroying the natural coolness of the underground chambers. These cave dwellings, completely furnished with the latest conveniences and furniture, capitalized on the traditional wisdom of times long before the advent of air-conditioning. Yet in the high-humidity climate of Japan this solution to summer heat could

never have been contemplated. Humid heat can only be mitigated by generating ventilation. In winter a masonry house in such a climate would be unbearably cold because of its high thermal capacity, and in summer it would only invite mold and mildew.

In parts of the dry zone in the Middle East and Africa, walls of sun-dried mud brick are often used in building homes even today. Since it is impossible to construct a roof out of mud bricks because of their fragility, these houses are usually roofed by building a network of interwoven branches over which woven straw or rush matting is laid and covered with mud or earth. In Iran, where earthquakes are frequent, whole communities are sometimes leveled by strong tremors, and there have been cases even in modern times where residents were buried alive in the collapsing earth and mud structure of their homes.

In this regard the earthquake resistant qualities of wood construction are far superior. The joints of a frame structure possess enough flexibility to absorb the energy of an earthquake. The resilient strength in a five-story wood-constructed pagoda made possible by the suspended central shaft, for example, cannot be duplicated in stone or brick. Another consideration is the heavy precipitation in most regions in Japan, necessitating an inclined roof to assure proper runoff. Construction of a sloped roof in stone or brick is very difficult, but with wood it is quite simple. By happy coincidence plentiful rainfall also speeds the growth of forests that provide lumber for construction.

Conditions of climate such as humidity and rainfall, as well as types of available building materials, have resulted in distinctive styles of dwellings in every country. The relationship between man and his dwelling has been consistent throughout history; in the warm and humid climate of Japan the wall is a secondary architectural element, while in the dry regions of the West it is primary. Even in today's industrial age these distinctive approaches provide the undercurrent in a modern architecture of reinforced steel and concrete, leaving an undeniable imprint on our townscapes.

Inside and Outside

In many parts of the world interior and exterior space seem to have a certain homogeneity. Attitudes and dress differ little depending on whether one is "inside" or "outside." In Italy, where masonry architecture prevails, floors and walls as well as streets are made of hard materials such as stone, giving inside and outside much the same physical appearance. This homogeneity of interior and exterior space is quite common in the world. One cultural trait that reveals much about the distinction, or lack of it, in perceptions of architectural space is in customs regarding footwear. Naturally, where masonry construction prevails, shoes are worn both inside and outside. In the warm climates of Southeast Asia and Africa the accepted custom is to go barefoot both inside and outside. Whether shoes are worn or not, most of the world's cultures view inside and outside space as equivalent. Japanese, however, maintain a sharp distinction between inside and outside, symbolized by the custom of removing shoes upon entering a home. This custom supports the clear, significant distinction between the two territories: the space where shoes are off is "inside," while the area where they are on is "outside." It is safe to say that most Japanese, when outside and wearing their shoes, feel an instinctive

sense of formality, which they shed only when they take off their shoes upon returning to the familiar, relaxed world of the home. One might add that this custom derives from the spatial order of their houses—an order symbolized by the architecture of the floor.

In recent years some urban dwellings in Japan have become so completely westernized—with comfortable living rooms filled with matching furniture and decor, bright and modern bathrooms and kitchens—that one might think himself transplanted to an apartment in New York or Scandinavia. Some Japanese homes measure up quite favorably to international standards of comfort and modernity, but an important and essential difference between residences in Japan and those in the West is that in the West a home may be considered basically part of the public external order of the city or the town, while in Japan it is a private, internal order. For a Japanese this interpretation helps explain why people in the West keep their shoes on inside just as they do outside, while in Japan the custom of taking them off is almost universal. Although having shoes on or off may seem a trivial matter, from the point of view of the territories of architectural space, it appears to have considerable significance.

There is an important difference between Japan and the West in conceptions of what is "internal" and what is "external." The philosopher Tetsurō Watsuji, author of a treatise on the Japanese and their environment, *Fūdo* ("Climate and Culture") written in 1939, early noted and described this difference in spatial consciousness:

Japanese customarily identify "house" with "inside." The world beyond its walls is "outside." On the "inside," distinctions between individuals cease to exist and the housewife calls her husband *uchi, uchi no hito,* or *taku,* all meaning literally, "the man of the house." He, like all the family members, *belongs* to the "inside." A man calls his wife *kanai,* literally, "woman in the house," and her role is defined by her presence in it. When speaking to outsiders, the members of one's family likewise are called "people of our household" (*uchi no mono*). The line between family members and those outside is clearly established, but within the household individual distinctions are largely ignored. Therefore a household is understood as a single entity consisting of undifferentiated relational contacts, an entity separate and distinct from the world outside. This distinction between inside and ouside is rather difficult to express in European terms. Although in western languages it is possible to refer to the "inside" and "outside" of a room, or of a house, there is no expression for "inside" and "outside" the relational bonds of the family. In the West pairs of expressions of corresponding importance are, first, the inside or outside of a person's mind, second, the inside and outside of a [physical] house, and, third, the inside and outside of the nation or the community/town. These evoke the dichotomy between spirit and body, man and nature, and man and community, but the dichotomy does not prevail in the standard view of family relationships. For Japanese the words "inside" and "outside" are a direct expression of human existence.[8]

The Japanese idea of "inside," then, is equivalent to "house," and the world beyond is "outside." In terms of spatial territory in architecture, inside is the space where one relaxes with shoes off, and outside is where one wears shoes and a formal demeanor.

To illustrate this with a very commonplace example, let us compare a western-style hotel to the Japanese-style resort hotel which has its roots in the traditional "Japanese inn" (*ryokan*). On the outside both types of hotels may be modern structures sturdily built of reinforced concrete. The spatial order within, however,

is entirely different, a difference created by distinct ways of establishing the boundary line between interior and exterior. First of all, as in the traditional inn, in the Japanese resort hotel guests remove their shoes at the entrance. Now, since Japanese ordinarily think of places where they remove their shoes as "internal space," they feel that the lobby, the corridors, and even the elevators are "internal space." Therefore it is perfectly permissible to stroll about in a comfortable cotton kimono in such areas, and no one feels the need to be properly and presentably dressed at all times. At night the front door of the Japanese inn-style hotel is locked, but individual rooms are often not locked. Personal activities such as bathing take place together with others in a spacious commmunal bathing room, often fitted with picture windows looking out on beautiful mountain or seaside landscapes. For Japanese, such an inn is the "internal space" of the home writ large, and they enjoy mingling with their fellow guests with the same ease and intimacy as they would with their own families.

By contrast, the so-called western-style hotel keeps its main entrance open twenty-four hours a day and shoes are worn in the lobby and the corridors. Unlike the Japanese-style hotel, it is spatially an extension of the outer spatial order of the street; in other words, it is public space. To those who consider the lobby and corridors of a hotel "external" space, people who dally in the hallways in bathrobe and slippers and chat freely with other guests are an annoyance. In a western hotel individual rooms are divided by solid walls and stout doors fitted with cleverly devised locks. Once inside one of these private rooms, a guest is in "internal space" and is free to take off his shoes and put on robe and bedroom slippers. Leaving this private room is equivalent to a Japanese to putting on his shoes and leaving his house.

From the Japanese point of view, the western rationale for distinguishing "internal" and "external" seems to be that, if you wear your shoes outside your bedroom, then, for example, the dining room of your own home and the dining hall of the hotel or the restaurant down the street are identical in that they are "outside" space. The western "shoes-on" atmosphere, in which one wears shoes inside, is one of an external spatial order premised on independence of individuals. The Japanese "shoes-off" atmosphere is a more intimate, internal, spatial order made up of undifferentiated individuals in a collectivity. I do not wish to suggest that the external order is necessarily better than the internal order. Unlike the external, the internal order imparts an intimacy and peace of mind that is much more conducive to comfort and closeness among those who live together. It is socially important to make a careful distinction between inside and outside, to know where to draw the line between internal and external spatial territories. For example, there may be people who consider a sleeping car or the corridors of a hotel "external space," while others consider these areas "internal space." If these two attitudes toward space should clash, and there were pronounced discrepancies in manner of dress, behavior, and conversation, unpleasantness would surely arise.

In Japan emphasis has traditionally been placed on the harmonious and aesthetically refined internal order of the home, a preoccupation that has meant a lack of concern, even a carelessness about external space. Maintaining attractiveness and order in public places has held little

interest. In the West, by contrast, the public square has been the focus of considerable attention since ancient times, as illustrated by the beautiful patterns of paving in the squares of many Italian cities. It is no coincidence that the custom of wearing shoes in the house emerged in the West, for the western way of life has its own concept of the external order. Tetsurō Watsuji observed several decades ago that activities that in Japan were customarily confined to the home are in the West traditionally carried on in public: one prays at church, relaxes in the park, eats in restaurants, and chats with friends and acquaintances in the public square.

University campuses, notorious for student demonstrations in the late sixties and early seventies, provide an interesting illustration of cultural differences in territorial space. In universities in the United States, the streets of the surrounding town often pass through the campus itself; you may find yourself on the campus one moment and in a residential section of the town the next. The university buildings face the street, each with its own numbered address. As a result an American university campus is an integral part of the town in which it is located, a kind of external space congruent with the external order. For security, however, it is of interest that American colleges invariably have their own special university police.

By contrast, Japanese university campuses are completely enclosed by a solid wall or fence, and access can be gained only through formal front, back, or side gates. If police, for example, who belong to the external order, intrude into this space, students and faculty react in much the same way as if their home had been invaded, because psychologically, for them the campus is internal space. When you enter a Japanese university campus you do not take off your shoes, but the feeling experienced as you enter its gates is quite the same as if you were removing your shoes at the front door of someone's home. In the university, as in the family, leadership is held by a paternal figure whose job is to ensure the peaceful and harmonious functioning of the internal order. In Japanese universities in the late sixties and early seventies, this leadership began to falter, and severe antagonism developed between administration and students. The administration, like the parents in a family, tried to resolve the conflict through a kind of familial understanding. The professors and students of a Japanese university, though their shoes were securely on, adopted the same patterns of behavior they would have in the shoes-off atmosphere of the home. From the point of view of the territories of architectural space, Japanese universities display an internal order; in this they are more like a Japanese-style inn than a western-style hotel.

As I said, the corridors and vestibules of western hotels and homes are extensions of the external spatial order, and guests enter with their shoes on because that space is not differentiated from the external order. If such spaces were unified under the Japanese internal order, it would be tantamount to going barefoot or in stocking feet in the streets or parks outside just as one would at home.

If Japanese do not think it is acceptable to walk barefoot outside, it is because they have a different way of integrating spatial territory. Again this has been aptly explained by Tetsurō Watsuji:

[In the West] one step out of one's room is little different from being in the family dining room, in a restaurant or out in the town. In other words, even the dining room of a home is "outside" in the Japanese sense of the term, and restaurants or opera houses play the role that sitting rooms or parlors might in Japanese homes. While, on the one hand, that which corresponds to the Japanese "home" may be little more than the area shut behind the door of an individual's room, on the other, the family circle in the Japanese sense extends in the West to the entire town or community. However, this is not an example of "relations without individual distinction" but of social interchange among distinct individuals. Yet even if "outside" means outside an individual's own room, in terms of the larger community it means "inside." The public parks of a town in the West are also traditionally "inside." One might say that what corresponds to a Japanese house and its surrounding fence in the West begins, on the one hand, at the very walls of an individual's bedroom and extends, on the other, to the city walls or the castle moat. Here the Japanese entranceway is equivalent to the main gate of a castle town. Therefore the houses that exist in the space between the "room" and the "castle walls" are not of such great significance.

. . . Japanese may have learned European ways of life on the surface, but, insofar as they remain bound by the household and cannot carry on a socially oriented life-style based on individualism, they can hardly claim to have become truly Europeanized. You may cover the streets with asphalt, but that doesn't mean that people will decide it is permissible to go out in their stocking feet. And even if shoes are worn inside, neither is anyone likely to think that shoes are to be worn on the almost sacred surface of *tatami* floors. In other words, who is there who would treat "inside the house" and "inside the town" in the same way? As long as the town is considered *outside* the household, the Japanese life-style cannot be considered "European."[9]

Japanese equate the house with "inside" and the streets with "outside," and there is no sense that these territories are integrated as in the West. By extension, such external space is unrelated to the individual or the internally oriented group;

it is an area "someone else" is responsible for. City space is considered "outside" and none of his concern. People may be meticulously tidy and attentive in keeping their surroundings in good taste as long as these pertain to internal space, but this does not lead them to feel any particular interest in areas such as streets, public squares, or parks. The western tradition of equal treatment for internal and external space, stimulated by ideas of city planning and street maintenance which began with the tradition of Leone Battista Alberti and others during the Renaissance, has encouraged the building of artistically beautiful cities, and many excellent examples remain in modern Europe. Lacking this tradition, for all their outstanding examples of private, secluded gardens and residences, Japanese cities evidence a visible apathy with regard to the attractiveness of the urban landscape.

Views from Within and Views from Without

Masonry construction in the West and post-and-beam construction in Japan's traditional architecture are also distinguished by completely different approaches to viewing the landscape. Gothic, Renaissance, and Baroque architecture, for instance, consist of heavy stone walls, dividing inside from outside into clearly distinct spaces. The exterior visage of the building itself bespeaks boldness, frontality, monumentality, and symmetry. It provides an impressive and satisfying appearance to be viewed from outside at some distance (figure 12). In terms of the relation of distance to building height (D/H), it is possible to get a proper appreciation of the building from the front if one is standing at a distance of more than two times the height of the building.[10] Meanwhile the interior spaces

of such buildings communicate a sense of majesty and solemnity. Yet, save for the sunshine that may be permitted to enter from tall slender windows, the internal space is independent, totally cut off from the streets outside. Both structural and spatial features make it relatively difficult to look out from the inside. Even if there is a garden adjacent to the building, it is usually independent of the interior and constitutes an exterior space all its own.

By contrast, in Japan the landscape surrounding a house is very often designed specifically to be viewed from inside. In traditional Japanese wood construction there are few permanent walls, and the intervals between the posts are generous, opening the inside of the house to its surroundings and bringing interior and exterior space into close association. This kind of architecture emphasizes the pleasure of viewing the garden landscape from a comfortable vantage point inside the house. Unlike architecture symbolized by the wall, that of the floor has few fixed walls; it more often than not lacks all pretense to monumentality, frontalism, or symmetry—qualities that would make it attractive as viewed from without. On the contrary, it is deliberately reticent, with its front entrance invariably out of sight beyond a winding pathway (figure 13).

In Kyoto there are some examples of traditional landscape gardens designed for strolling, such as those of Katsura Detached Palace and the Shūgakuin Imperial Villa, but the most common are small-scale, secluded gardens intended primarily to be viewed from within the adjacent temple or residence for which they were designed. Such views are often enhanced by "framing" through careful attention to the surrounding woodwork and translucent *shōji*, whose design contributes to the total effect. A masterful example of this

12
Frontality, the view
from without of Notre-
Dame, Paris
(Photograph: Yoshinobu
Ashihara)

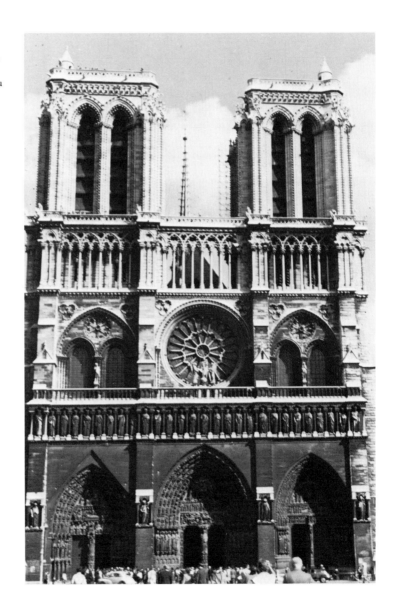

13
Antithesis of frontality,
Katsura Detached Palace
lying secluded beyond
a winding path
(Photograph: Yukio
Futagawa)

14
View from within the
Bōsen-no-ma, Kohōan,
Daitokuji
(Photograph: Akio
Kawasumi)

compositional technique may be found in the Bōsen-no-ma in the Kohōan at Daitokuji temple (figure 14). In this room the upper portion of the opening facing the garden is filled with a *shōji* panel that interrupts the line of vision and guides it downward, focusing attention on the stone water basin close at hand and the stone lantern, with only a glimpse of the small encircling garden. While a quite simple technique, the effect of this design is very striking. Another excellent example of the framed landscape is at Katsura Detached Palace (figure 15). There the view from within the Ni-no-ma of the Ko-shoin extends beyond the moon-viewing platform that forms the veranda. The large rectangular opening extending from floor to ceiling is framed by a vertically slatted transom and translucent *shōji* panels at both sides. Below, the bamboo moon-viewing platform reaches out to the pond, where on a promontory a stone pagoda just enters the range of vision. With the full moon shining over this pond in midautumn, there is perhaps no more exquisite landscape than that viewed from inside this room.

Another famous garden designed to be viewed from within is the stone garden at Ryōanji temple (figure 16). Believed to have been designed and built around the late fifteenth century, it is a flat (*hiraniwa*), dry landscape (*karesansui*) garden featuring an arrangement of fifteen stones. It occupies an area 10 meters wide and 24 meters long, bounded on three sides by a low earthen wall and in front by the veranda of the temple. The arrangement of the stones has inspired many theories about its design, and each person who sees it comes away with a different impression and understanding. The earthen wall is an important boundary element delineating the territory of the garden. It is a space carved out of the natural landscape beyond, but incorporating it by means of a technique in Japanese landscape gardening known as "borrowed scenery" (*shakkei*). The full effect of gardens designed like this can be captured only from within buildings. If one were to stand in the garden itself, the landscape would seem meaningless and aesthetically unappealing. The philosophical symbolism and mystic significance of the Ryōanji stone garden, in particular, are completely lost if not viewed from within. Among many more of these inner gardens in Kyoto is that of the Shisendō temple (figure 17), previously the residence of a poet and connoisseur of the tea ceremony of the early Tokugawa period.

Japanese homes and temples often contain very small inner gardens known as *tsuboniwa* (figure 18). These gardens are not meant to be entered; they are, rather, miniature landscapes intended to be viewed from the adjacent rooms. The smaller of these are around 3 meters square, and the larger as much as 10 meters square. One may happen upon such gardens in temples, in private homes, or in traditional-style inns or restaurants in Kyoto. They may even occasionally be found in large-scale modern architecture, to be enjoyed from surrounding rooms (figure 19).

The Japanese technique of *bonsai*, in which trees and shrubs are cultivated by dwarfing natural plants, carries the landscape to be viewed from within to an extreme of miniaturization. Like the *tsuboniwa*, they represent techniques Japanese have refined to reduce the vastness of nature to a manageable size and introduce it into interior space, where it can be appreciated from within.

15
Framed view from
inside the Ni-no-ma,
Ko-shoin, Katsura
Detached Palace
(Photograph: Yoshinobu
Ashihara)

16
Stone garden, Ryōanji
(Photograph: Yoshinobu
Ashihara)

17
Shisendō temple garden
viewed from inside
(Photograph: Akio
Kawasumi)

18
Tsuboniwa, Myōshinji,
Kyoto
(Photograph: Haruzō
Ōhashi)

19
Inner garden of the Dai-
ichi Kangyō Bank
building, Tokyo,
Yoshinobu Ashihara,
architect
(Photograph: Seiichirō
Tanaka)

20
Building exterior in the
Shibuya quarter of
Tokyo
(Photograph: Yoshinobu
Ashihara)

Why is the landscape as viewed from
within so important in Japan? Naturally
climatic factors and considerations of local
culture may explain this particular preference, but I would suggest that it is also
because Japanese residences are governed
by an architecture of the inside that is
oriented to the floor. The floor is conceived of as a pure, "sanctified" space
demarcated from the surrounding environment. In terms of the hierarchy of
space, it represents a higher spatial order
raised above ground level and incorpo-
rates a yet higher step in the *tokonoma*, an
alcove for the display of fine art objects.
It is from this elevated position inside
that the landscape outside is intended to
be viewed.

The view from without in Japan takes
second place to the view from within. In
fact it is often summarily dismissed as a
matter of concern in building design. In
other words, the sensitive treatment accorded to interior space does not extend
to thinking with regard to the exterior
order as called for in modern urban
planning.

Nowhere is this lack of concern for exterior space so well demonstrated as in
the downtown areas of large cities such as
Tokyo or Osaka. There, walls are plastered with posters and neon advertising
signs from side to side, and rooftops are
crowned with immense advertising towers
(figures 20 and 21). How is it that Japanese, so attentive to the design of exquis-
itely beautiful interior spaces, end up with
such unsightly building exteriors? The
only explanations I can find are in the
priority given interior over exterior space
that arises from the attitude toward garden scenery viewed from within and the
characteristics of the "architecture oriented to the floor."

The layout of public parks in Japanese cities, however, seems to be influenced by a principle of garden design that assumes they are meant to be viewed from inside. When landscape designers plan a park in the city, they traditionally seek to create autonomous spaces that are territorially complete in themselves. To achieve this effect, they encircle the park with huge trees or fences or walls which will cut it off from the surrounding city. There are many famous examples of such secluded gardens in Tokyo alone, including the Shinjuku Imperial Gardens, the Koishikawa Botanical Gardens, and Rikugi-en, a classical estate garden converted into a public park. The enclosing walls of these gardens provide tranquil, secluded spaces protected from the noise and commotion of the streets outside.

There are some examples of semisecluded gardens in Tokyo, one of which is Hibiya Park. Although situated in the heart of downtown Tokyo, this park has somehow not completely captured the affections of city residents and commuters. For people passing by in automobiles along the broad avenues that encircle the park, all that is visible is a dense growth of evergreen trees. The inside is completely hidden. The dense ring of trees makes the park, in terms of territorial space, a self-contained, introverted space with a centripetal order. For those who happen to walk into it, the park offers a kind of unexpected oasis in the midst of the city. The semisecluded garden technique is well suited, however, to naturally wooded parks extending over large areas such as New York's Central Park, Paris's Bois de Bologne, and Rome's Villa Borghese; Hibiya Park is actually too small for this purpose. Its area is only 500 meters from north to south, 290 meters from east to west at one point, and 330

21
Building exteriors in the Shibuya quarter of Tokyo
(Photograph: Yoshinobu Ashihara)

22
Idea for redesign of
Hibiya Park
(From *Machinami no
bigaku*)

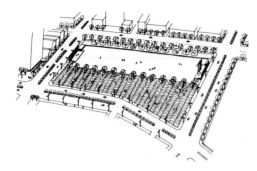

meters at its widest point. The space
might have been more beneficially used
had it been designed to be more open
and integrated with the surrounding city.

One way of dealing with this problem
might be to lay an attractively patterned
pavement on a 100-meter-wide strip
along the east side of the park to provide
a pleasant promenade like those built
along the coasts of the Copacabana in Rio
de Janeiro in Brazil. A section of the park
along the promenade could be made into
a pond, and as in New York's Rockefeller
Center this could be converted in winter
into a no-charge ice skating rink. The rest
of the year it would revert to a shallow
pond imparting a refreshing, cool atmosphere. The western edge of the park,
which is 500 meters long, could be given
over to the display of outdoor sculpture
(figure 22). The city could offer this space
to young artists from all over the world
to exhibit their works, as the area can
accommodate a large number.

Cities with Walls
The concept of the wall and the floor as
defining architectural space in masonry
and post-and-beam architecture extends
to the structure of cities: one develops in
orientation to the wall, the other to the
floor. The significance of this difference
first struck me some twenty years ago
when I visited in the province of Tuscany
the fortified cities of Assisi and San
Gimignano, imposing stone fortresses
built atop broad hills in medieval times.
For an architect, a walled city like these is
equivalent to one large, integrated building.

San Gimignano's distinctive towers are
visible many miles away. At the portals of
the city its ramparts rise up sharply several meters, but entering the gates is like

passing through the front door of a private residence (figure 23). The main gate is one of several entrances, reminiscent of the front, back, and side doors of a house. Inside, a narrow winding street connects the main gate to the center of the town, crowded on both sides with stone houses, cheek-by-jowl. Above are glimpses between the rooftops of the tower that is the symbol of the town. Progressing along the corridorlike street, one emerges suddenly into a broad square—the Piazza della Cisterna and the adjoining Piazza del Duomo. In both, the former focused on the city's main well and the latter on the church, there is not a tree in sight. Stone is everywhere, from the walls of the surrounding buildings to the floor of the fully paved piazza. It is said that Italians have the largest living rooms in the world, and these broad piazzas are clearly spacious extensions of the living rooms of the city residents. The people visit the square many times a day to chat with friends, relax, watch their children play, and on Sundays to attend church and socialize.

Later I visited many other small cities in the southern region of Apulia—Alberobello, Locorotondo, Martina Franca, Cisternino—and many of the islands that dot the Aegean Sea—Hydra, Patmos, Mikonos, Santorini—and found that one- and two-story residential districts in the Mediterranean area are generally centripetally ordered spaces facing inward from a circumscribing boundary. Although simple in design, they demonstrate a surprising variety and order. Inside the fortifications, these towns present an "internal order" not unlike that which characterizes the Japanese home. Along their winding streets, white-painted stone buildings stand silhouetted against the blue of sky

23
Gateway to San
Gimignano, Italy
(Photograph: Yoshinobu
Ashihara)

and sea beyond, and bits of the outside world peek through and over the walls. Within, there is a strong sense of the human warmth and intimacy with nature that the highly industrialized twentieth-century society is gradually losing.

Yet the townscape that unfolds within this walled city, so like a single, self-contained composite building, is one most Japanese would find quite alien. The urban spatial order tends to go in an opposite direction from cities in Japan. A city like San Gimignano consciously orients itself to the wall; it is an inward-turned, centripetal order ruled by the wall. The cities in Japan, meanwhile, demonstrate a centrifugal order ruled by the floor, which produces an urban sprawl directed outward, totally oblivious to boundaries.

Why is is that walled towns developed in other regions of the globe, but not in Japan? The reason, I believe, is closely connected with the meaning of a "wall" as an architectural phenomenon and with the tendency to either affirm or to disclaim the wall in architectural styles. Walled cities are located primarily in the dry zone, and, although this hypothesis warrants further scholarly study, we can intuitively sense that the walled city is closely associated with dry climates.[11] Japanese philosopher Watsuji observed this phenomenon in his book on climate and culture:

In a dry climate, thirst is the ruling force. Life is devoted to the constant pursuit of water and to guarding the source of water for the group. A tribe's very existence may be imperiled if its water source falls into the hands of another tribe . . . and because of these two facts of life, desert man is both aggressive and combative by nature.[12]

The history of dry regions, in fact, is one of continuous conflict. In this kind of habitat man cannot depend on nature; he must struggle for even the barest subsistence. It is a struggle with nature, as Watsuji suggests, that eventually leads man into conflict with his fellow man. A way of life in which antagonism is implicit, in turn, fosters solidarity among tribal groups. Group solidarity was fostered in ancient times by the castle walls or the ramparts of a walled city, the "boundary line" that provided the demarcation between inside and outside and made self-defense possible. The purpose of a walled city is not only to protect against the intrusions of outside enemies but to mark the territory of the group. Lewis Mumford writes in his book, *The Culture of Cities*:

Though the wall existed for military defense and the main ways of the city were usually planned to facilitate rallying to the main gates, the psychological import of the wall must not be forgotten. One was either in or out of the city; one belonged or one did not belong. When the town gates were locked at sundown, and the portcullis was drawn, the city was insulated from the ouside world. As in a ship, the wall helped create a feeling of unity between the inhabitants: in a siege or a famine the morality of the shipwreck— share-and-share-alike—developed easily.[13]

In the walled cities of the West the whole town is fortified. In the medieval wars no mercy was shown to women and children, and families and even livestock were located and guarded within the castle walls. There are "castle towns" in Japan, but the contrast between these and their European counterparts is striking. The residences of the vassals of a Japanese lord were built immediately surrounding the castle, while the townspeople lived on the fringes of the town. Only the castle proper was fortified by a wall (figure 24). The significance of the castle was far more important as a symbol of power than as a functional defense

24
Himeji Castle, Hyōgo
prefecture
(Photograph: Yukio
Futagawa)

25
Castle towns in Europe
and Japan
(From *Machinami no
bigaku*)

Inhabitants

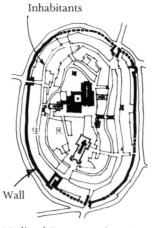

Wall

Medieval European city

Inhabitants

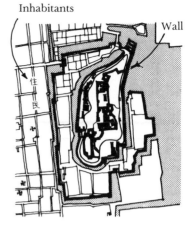

Wall

Japanese castle town

Inhabitants

Diagram of medieval
European city

Diagram of medieval
Japanese city

in battle. In this kind of town the people of a desert heritage as in southern Europe and the Middle East would not have felt secure even for a day. A diagram of these two types of cities (figure 25) shows that the fortifications and the residential areas of the towns are in reverse figure-ground configuration. For the people of the dry zone the way castles were built in Japan would seem totally unrealistic, almost like something out of a fairy tale. But Japanese, by the same token, find the impregnable walled city just as unrealistic and unnecessary.

Nevertheless, for man to be able to live with a feeling of security, the existence of some kind of boundary in space is a necessity. For Japanese who live in thin-walled houses in unfortified urban settlements, then, what is it that fulfills this need? Perhaps, because Japanese live in an island country situated at considerable distance from the Asian continent and separated from it by a broad stretch of water once crossed only with difficulty, and because they are in general of homogeneous character and culture, the boundary that exists in their subconscious is in fact the ocean that surrounds the islands, fortifying the country like an immense moat. In place of the man-made fortresses that desert peoples of the dry zone constructed around their territories, Japanese were provided with a natural geographical boundary in the form of the ocean, a boundary remote from the consciousness of having been created by man. For continental peoples of different religions and different ethnic groups, words like *kaigai* (overseas) and *gaikoku* (literally, "outside countries"), which suggest places beyond such an ocean boundary, do not have the same meaning as they do for Japanese. Viewed from abroad, Japan

must appear to be a solidly unified group living within an island fortress provided by the surrounding oceans. Certainly, the way people outside Japan view it springs largely from their different orientation to the concept of a "boundary."

2

*Composition of
the Townscape*

Buildings and Streets

In the history of cities the awareness of and affection for streets is strongest in the Latin countries of western Europe and conspicuously weak in Japan. Italians in particular make the street an integral part of their daily life. For them it exists not simply to carry traffic but as a central arena of the community. Bernard Rudofsky notes that the porticos of Bologna provide much more than shelter from the elements, they are the site of a time-honored custom:

The Bolognese, running back and forth under the colonnades all day long, still would not want to miss the formal promenade that takes place twice a day opposite the Dome under the Portico del Pavaglione. At noon and in the early evening hours, large crowds mill through this vastest of the city's corridors, and it is impossible *not* to meet one's friends.[1]

Clearly the street is a crucial element of the Italian way of life and an expression of the bonds among the inhabitants of its cities. Rudofsky goes on to note that the English are rather less attached to their streets:

Surely, the English are not a desirable model for an urban society. No other nation developed such a fierce devotion to country life as they did. And with good reason; their cities have been traditionally among Europe's least wholesome. Englishmen may be intensely loyal to their towns, but the street—the very gauge of urbanity—does not figure large in their affections. By preference, they take refuge in the beery atmosphere of the pub. Lord Tennyson spoke for the many when he declaimed: "I loath the squares and streets/And the faces that one meets."[2]

The piazza is an urban open space loved by Italians specifically for meeting people. The English park, on the other hand, is intended for solitary relaxation. In Japan exterior spaces like parks or squares have historically held little interest. Interior space was treated with great refinement and aesthetic sensitivity, but the same sophistication did not extend to exterior space.

When a traveler finds himself in a new city, the first thing he looks for is a map, one that will provide a detailed guide to the names of the streets and squares. As Jane Jacobs has written: "Think of a city, and what comes to mind? Its streets. If a city's streets look interesting, the city looks interesting; if they look dull, the city looks dull."[3] Indeed, the streets are the scale upon which a traveler judges a city. The French word *rue* and the Italian word *via* have their own particular associations, invoking the image of a city and arousing the itch to travel.

The names of streets are important, inseparable attributes of the life of a city. And yet in Japan streets are seldom named, save in a few cities like Kyoto, planned and endowed with pleasant street names in ancient times, or Sapporo, built more recently, which has a New York-style numbering system based on the cardinal directions. In most Japanese cities it is customary to indicate an address by reference to numbers corresponding to established community areas or blocks. The practice of naming on the basis of an *area* rather than a street derives from the same thinking that produced the architecture of the floor. In Europe, where architectural concepts are oriented to the wall, it follows quite reasonably that addresses be indicated for houses numbered in linear succession along the streets upon which they face. The Japanese practice of naming and numbering in terms of discrete areas is quite unusual in the world today. Its strong orientation to the block or area unit, rather than to the street, again demonstrates the deeply rooted consciousness

of inside versus outside and of architecture as stemming from the "floor."

As a general rule building sites face directly on a street. The composition and character of a townscape take shape from the spatial conception and design of the boundary area adjoining the street. Let us examine, then, how the relationship of streets and buildings in urban space determines the townscape.

Some years ago I lived for a period of time in the beautiful residential area along the harbor in Sydney, Australia, known as Rose Bay. This is an area dominated by one- or at most two-story private homes, separated from the street by carefully manicured lawns and colorful flowerbeds. Their meticulously tended gardens seem to be intended more for people passing by than for the residents themselves, for the front yards are largely hidden from view inside the houses but open and plainly visible from the street, contributing generally to the attractiveness of the entire neighborhood. This suburban, "garden-city" style of townscape is typical of residential areas all over the United States and in parts of Europe. I remember with particular fondness the streets of suburban Honolulu, where there is a striking stretch from the Waikiki area to Kahala Avenue passing in front of Diamond Head. Lush lawns stretch back from wide sidewalks and flowering trees and shrubs are scattered across the lawns and around the houses (figures 26 and 27).

In the residential areas of Japan's major cities, by contrast, space that corresponds to a front yard visible from the street is extremely rare. The houses, most of which are built in the traditional style of wooden post-and-beam construction, are so open that some kind of surrounding wall seems necessary both for privacy

Front yard
(external order)

Sidewalk

Grass

Street

and safety. If the site has a north entrance, the garden will invariably be on the south and therefore difficult to see from the street. If the site has a south entrance, there will be a high wall so that the bedroom and living room are not exposed to the street. Thus, even if there is a garden, it is seldom visible and plays a negligible role in the townscape (figures 28 and 29)

Let us now explore the differences between the front yards of the western townscape and the gardens of Japanese houses in terms of the territories of space. While in both cases the entire site obviously belongs to the owner of the house, in the western-style residence, it would appear that the front yard is consciously included in the external, public order rather than the internal, private one. In other words, in terms of spatial territory, the front yard is conceived of as part of the street. In Japan, on the other hand, the garden is consciously part of the private, internal order belonging to the resident. A wall provides an explicit dividing line between the public and the private spaces, indicating that the garden is not intended to make a contribution to the composition of the townscape. Because of this the townscapes of Japanese residential areas, even those occupied by the wealthy, seem much less attractive than the open atmosphere of western-style residential areas.

Let us look, however, at a type of townscape that is fundamentally different from either of these examples. In Greece and Italy houses are generally of stone masonry construction, and built directly on the street; there are no front yards. Any left-over ground surface around the stone buildings is paved and used as part of the street. The street is determined by the shape of the buildings, now opening wide, now becoming narrow, turning at odd angles, and intersecting itself as it pleases (figures 30 and 31).

At first, one might think these streets are quite the same as the expressionless, walled-in streets of Japan. Yet the exterior walls of houses, unlike the fences that line Japan's streets, have doors and windows that promote continuity between inside and outside, permitting the scene of human activity to overflow into the street. This is part of the delightful flavor of these townscapes, inhabited by ordinary, simple folk. The spatial structure is completely different from that of the western "garden-city" townscape with its suburban-style front yards, and yet it, too, presents a richly human quality. In spots where the street widens, people stop and talk as they would in a square; they put out chairs to do their mending, and relax in the cool of the evening. In terms of the territories of space, this demonstrates how the private, internal order of the home permeates the outer, public order of the street in the form of regular daily activities like mending and evening relaxation. In other words, the street is partly included in the internal order. In a townscape of the garden-city type with its front yards, the external order of the street permeates the internal order; in that of Greece and Italy, it is the reverse, the internal order flowing out into the external one. Both townscapes have their advantages and disadvantages, but they are especially memorable for their attractiveness and human warmth.

Another type of townscape is that which contains patios or inner gardens, as found in Spain or the Islamic countries. Spain's townscapes generally resemble those of Greece or southern Italy. They have an atmosphere of remarkable unity, with brownish-yellow Spanish roof tiles

28
Typical urban residential
townscape in Japan
(Photograph: Yoshinobu
Ashihara)

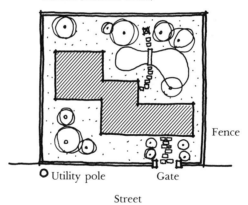

29
Typical layout of urban
residential townscape in
Japan

30
Residential townscape in
Italy
(Photograph: Yoshinobu
Ashihara)

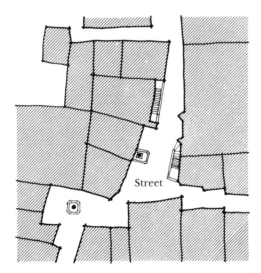

Street

31
Italian townscape with
no leftover space
between streets and
buildings

used throughout and walls painted white with lime. Unlike Italy, outdoor activities of a private nature take place in the courtyards of each home, so the streets are not so necessary as a forum of activity. In fact, save for the bright foliage and plants hung on the walls around the inner gardens that may be glimpsed through the open gateways, these streets seem quite desolate.

Japan, too, has townscapes composed of houses built directly on the street. Some well-known examples are the townhouses of Kyoto, the inns of Tsumago, and the shops of Hida Takayama. Today these townscapes, whose character has been preserved for generations, are gaining new recognition. On close inspection the individual buildings are somewhat different, but the use of common building techniques and carpentry imparts a sense of unity and shared values that sustains the whole. A townscape in the true sense is one brought into being by common qualities, and it is on that basis that a town or community establishes itself in the affections of its residents.

The townhouses of Kyoto front right on the streets and contribute to the townscape with wonderfully functional, as well as attractive, wooden lattices that mark the boundary between the street and the buildings. These lattices impart a sense of fluidity between the inner and outer order and help to animate the townscape in much the same way as do the doors and windows of the buildings in Italy. Visually, the lattice functions like a one-way mirror, in that it is possible to see from the dark side to the light side but not vice versa. During the day one can see the street from within the houses, but from outside it is difficult to see inside.

Where the vertical bars are made more rectangular in depth, the lattice is stronger and more concealing (figure 32). These lattices link the houses to the streets before them, protecting the privacy of the residents, on the one hand, and fostering close community relations on the other.

The typical townhouses of Kyoto are located on streets 6.5 meters wide, and their average height is 5 meters, so the distance/height (D/H) ratio equals 1.3. These proportions of the exterior space conform to the human scale, a scale in which one immediately feels at home. The streets of Kyoto are straight and 90 meters or less in length, and anything that happens there is easily visible.[4] As a townscape whose design promotes an intermingling of internal and external orders and a sense of community, Kyoto is an outstanding example. Children playing out in the street are within their mothers's sight through the wooden lattices; daily activities and events—sweeping, care of potted plants, sprinkling the streets to keep down the dust, and passing festival processions—make the street a lively place where children grow up in immediate contact with society and the physical world outside the home.

In every country, as industrialization advances, the attachments that grow out of a sense of community are gradually fading. Young people increasingly choose the anonymity and impersonality of big city living to eschew the watchful eyes of close neighbors. In Japan residential areas are filling with huge company apartment complexes, where the corporate organizational hierarchy reaches out even to the home life of employees, and public housing complexes, where people must dwell in concrete boxes situated in a townscape they can have no voice or role in creating. Many societal problems arise when children grow and develop in inhuman

urban environments such as these. Careful thought must be given to how, despite the growing dehumanization of contemporary society, we can restore a truly human way of life and how we can make more attractive and liveable the urban environments in which we live.

D/H and W/D Proportions of the Townscape

An important aspect of townscape composition depends on the ratio of street width to building height. Let us examine these proportions, using D for the distance between buildings on both sides of the street and H for the height of the adjacent buildings. My observations have shown that $D/H = 1$ may be taken as a kind of median from which spatial qualities vary depending on whether D/H is greater or less than 1. As D/H rises above 1, the space opens up, and, as it passes 2, gradually becomes expansive or vast. When D/H falls below 1, space grows increasingly intimate, until eventually it is simply cramped. When D/H equals 1, a balance is achieved; for actual building purposes D/H ratios of about 1, 2, or 3 are the most feasible (figure 33).

In the medieval walled cities of Italy, where the premium on space makes the streets very narrow, the D/H ratio is approximately 0.5, although street width is very irregular. The streets of Renaissance cities were comparatively wide; Leonardo da Vinci believed that a width equal to the height of surrounding buildings (so that $D/H = 1$) was the ideal proportion. The Baroque era reversed the proportions of medieval times, introducing streets twice as wide as the height of buildings, $D/H = 2$ (figure 34).[5] To this day in the back alleys of Italian cities narrow $D/H \approx$ 0.5 streets prevail, and laundry hung from lines suspended between windows

of buildings facing each other is a common sight (figure 35). In Japan the traditional townhouses that make up certain dense neighborhoods in Kyoto are built on a $D/H = 1.3$ ratio, exemplifying comfortable space on a human scale.

Modern architects have relied on the concept of D/H since the turn of the century to calculate proportions that will ensure sunlight and privacy (figure 36), but they have not used it consciously as a technique in townscape design. The usual distance between buildings represents a D/H ratio of 1, 2, or 3, although Le Corbusier often employed a D/H of 5 and sometimes close to 10. This practice of making buildings monumental "figures" in the Gestalt scheme was not conducive to the concept of D/H, which is part of an approach that treats interbuilding space as "figure" in the manner of Camillo Sitte. It was only natural that Le Corbusier disapproved of Sitte, for they emphasized different things. Sitte, had he been a contemporary of Le Corbusier, would undoubtedly have criticized the latter for his penchant for monumentality and his inattention to the street. As an architect, I do not consider D/H the supreme principle of modern architectural design, but it is valuable as a demonstration of the Gestalt phenomenon in the composition of exterior space, particularly in complexes of separate structures such as housing developments, townscapes, and urban environments.

In Japan's townscapes where narrow streets are crowded along both sides with small stores, there is a variety, rhythm, and bustling atmosphere distinctive of Asia. There are many well-known examples, such as the back streets of Shibuya or Shinjuku in Tokyo and Motomachi or Chinatown in Yokohama. Analysis of such streets shows that this characteristically

33
D/H relationship in
architecture

When *D/H* = 1, a balance is achieved
between height and distance

When *D/H* < 1, the space
grows crowded and cramped

As *D/H* grows larger, the space becomes more open

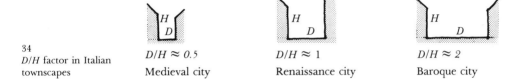

34
D/H factor in Italian
townscapes

D/H ≈ 0.5
Medieval city

D/H ≈ 1
Renaissance city

D/H ≈ 2
Baroque city

35
Back streets of Italy
where $D/H < 0.5$
(Photograph: Yoshinobu
Ashihara)

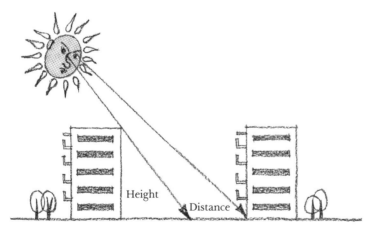

36
D/H as a way of
checking sunlight
between buildings

Height

Distance

Asian atmosphere of crowded bustle exists only in streets less than 20 to 25 meters wide. As explained by my exterior modular theory in *Exterior Design in Architecture*, this width coincides with the 70- to 80-foot distance at which a human face can be readily identified.[6]

In addition to the ratio $D/H \geqq 1$ we can see that the width (W) of the shop-fronts with relation to the breadth of the street (D) is also important in describing the townscape. Motomachi Street has such a desirable ratio, at about $W/D = 0.6$, where W equals the width of one store front (figures 37 and 38). The series of stores whose W proportion is shorter than D gives the townscape its characteristic Asian animation. A large facade built on such a narrow street fails to foster this effect; if absolutely necessary, the use of a series of accents can make it appear to conform with the $W/D < 1$ proportion.

This concept of W/D may be illustrated using the Palazzo Uffizzi of Florence designed by Giorgio Vasari (figure 39). Its courtyard has a $D/H \approx 0.6$, giving it a sense of enclosure, and the rows of columns create a feeling of rhythm and unity that enlivens the exterior space. If one were to apply a ratio of $W/D = 1$ to the Uffizzi, it would look more modern (figure 40), and a ratio of $W/D = 0.6$ would give it an atmosphere of Asiatic bustle (figure 41).

The Gestalt Phenomenon in Exterior Space

In 1954 I visited Italy for the first time. As I stood in the squares of its medieval cities, I experienced an unexpected thrill. While out-of-doors, I felt as though I were indoors, standing within a huge hall that lacked only a roof. It may have been the good Italian wine, but I could not escape the sensation that the roofs of the

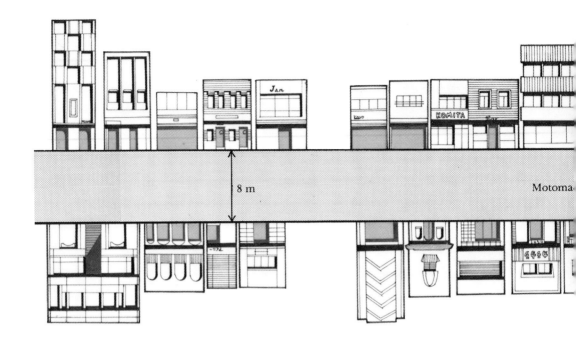

8 m

Motoma

37
Plan and elevations of
Motomachi Street,
Yokohama

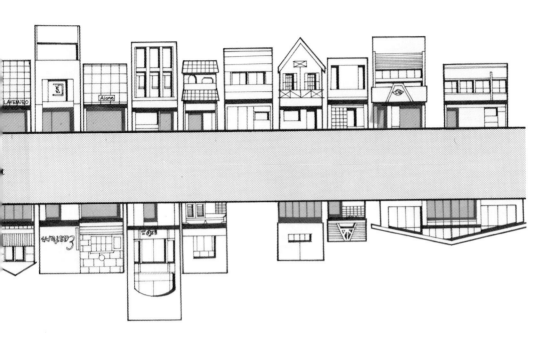

38
Motomachi Street,
Yokohama
(Photograph: Sumiho
Ōta)

39
Palazzo Uffizi, Florence
(Photograph: Yoshinobu
Ashihara)

40
Palazzo Uffizi imagined
in modern style

41
Palazzo Uffizi made
"Asiatic"

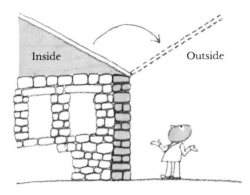

Inside   Outside

42
Sensation of inside and
outside reversal one
experiences in the
Italian piazza

adjacent houses extended over the square and that exterior and interior space had been uncannily reversed (figure 42). Then again, perhaps the illusion resulted from my excitement at the experience of seeing genuine examples of the "architecture of the wall," essentially for the first time. As a Japanese, I was accustomed to the "architecture of the floor" in which interior and exterior spaces are practically antithetical. In Italy inside and outside spaces struck me as homogeneous, almost interchangeable.

In the late fifties the principles of Gestalt psychology began to be applied not only to the perception of two-dimensional forms but to three-dimensional spaces of the city and its architecture. Although it still remains debatable, Gestalt theory has been found applicable to architecture, first, as demonstrated in the theories of Steen Eiler Rasmussen and, later, by Christian Norberg-Schulz and the school of contextualism. The sense of inversion of interior and exterior space I experienced in the Italian square had actually been an encounter with the phenomenon of figure-ground reversal as illustrated by Edgar Rubin's vase-faces figure (figure 68, chapter 3). The exterior space of Italian streets and squares, in other words, is homogeneous with the interior of adjacent architectural space and therefore possesses the qualities of figure. My experience confirmed the existence of Gestalt qualities in Italian exterior space.

Now, if we probe deeper into the theory of figure and ground, we may find in it a kinship with yin and yang, which have been part of Chinese thought since ancient times. The Chinese believed that the essence of things was an elusive, undefined and imperceptible emptiness, and this they called *ch'i* (Japanese, *ki*). This emptiness is the basis of life and the vital force of the universe, and it can be expressed in the coexistence of yin and yang. The myriad things of the universe are manifested in yin and yang and these two principles in turn exist in everything.[7]

The Chinese philosopher Lao Tzu explained the relative perceptions of the concepts of "something" and "nothing" as being closely associated to yin-yang thought. He observed that, "Though clay may be molded into a vase, the essence of the vase is in the emptiness within it." In empty, undefined space, if one draws a circle, the space within the circle is set apart from empty space and a converging space created. In other words, it becomes yang, a space demarcated from yin; it is *something*, separate from the surrounding nothingness. In order to become yang, or something, there must be a boundary which will form an entity, a substance that functions as the borderline of a figure.

But Lao Tzu spoke of something and nothing only with regard to one discrete object—a vase. When there is only one vase in question, his point is clear, the space inside it is *something*—limited, "positive space"—while that outside it is undefined emptiness—or negative space (figure 43a). On the other hand, if there are two vases, though there is *P*-space within each of the vases, in the space between the two a quality emerges which is also akin to *something*; we may call it positive-negative (*PN*) space (figure 43b). Say, a number of vases are gathered into a circle; then a situation equivalent to the inside and outside of an individual vessel emerges. The space encircled by the vessels becomes defined—it is *something*, or positive space—and that outside them is *nothing*, or negative space (figure 43c). Now, if we think of these vessels as individual buildings, we can envision a space

(a)

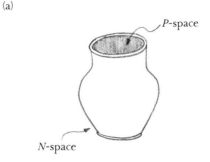

(b)

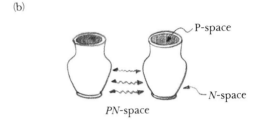

(c)

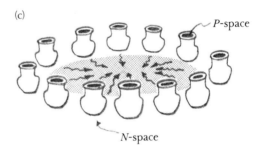

43
Positive space formed
by several surrounding
entities

such as the Italian square surrounded by architecture as being equivalent to "figure" in the Gestalt sense.

In Italy, a street is not considered a street unless it is lined on both sides by houses standing close together. In fact the most pleasing qualities of Italian towns are the continuity and rhythm created by the even positioning of buildings, not unlike the attractive smile of a person with even teeth. Just as a decayed tooth or a shiny gold denture totally alters a person's features, when a house on such a street is torn down and replaced with some new discordant structure, it destroys the aesthetic equilibrium.

Bernard Rudofsky writes that the street

... cannot exist in a vacuum; it is inseparable from its environment. In other words, it is no better than the company of houses it keeps. The street is the matrix: urban chamber, fertile soil, and breeding ground. Its viability depends as much on the right kind of architecture as on the right kind of humanity. The perfect street is harmonious space. Whether it is confined by the near-hermetic houses of an African Kasbah or by Venetian filigree marble palaces, what counts is the continuity and rhythm of its enclosure. One might say that the street is a street by courtesy of the buildings that line it. Skyscrapers and empty lots do not a city make.[8]

A close look at the maps of old Italian towns shows that all the streets and public squares are carefully delineated and paved to the base of the building walls that surround them, leaving no ambiguous or undefined spaces between buildings and street area. Thus a negative print of the map (figure 44) is as clear and meaningful as a positive print.

In Japan, by contrast, houses do not necessarily completely fill the sites in which they are situated; left-over space frequently remains, necessitating fences or hedges to maintain privacy. A map of old Edo (Tokyo before 1868), then, is merely a sketch of building sites showing the relation of sites to street, and the relationship of buildings to street is not clear. A negative print of such a map (figure 45) does not display a meaningful example of the Gestalt phenomenon.

A negative of the map of an Italian city, however, effectively reverses the figure-ground scheme, producing the same result as Edgar Rubin's vase-faces figure. The clear outline of streets and squares sustains the figure effect, and this is made possible because structures are built closely on both sides of the streets and bordering immediately on them. The streets in these cities perform an equally important role in daily life as do the buildings, and certain aspects of life are inextricably associated with street space. If the buildings are solitary or monumental structures, they naturally dominate and assume the role of figure, while the streets become the space or ground that fills in the empty space.

A beautiful example of the Renaissance-style square is the Piazza Ducale (figure 46) in the small town of Vigevano northwest of Milan. Its design has been variously attributed to Leonardo da Vinci, Bramante, and Antonio Filarete, but Paul Zucker states that it was actually built between 1492 and 1498 by Ambrogio di Curtis with the cooperation of Leonardo and Bramante.[9] To stand in this square is to experience vividly the quality of spatial unity that Zucker believes is typical of the Italian Renaissance piazza. The continuity and cohesiveness derives from the uniform roof and eave lines, the regular shapes of the windows in the buildings along its three sides, as well as from the $D/H \approx 4$ ratio of the structures on the shorter side of the square. The double arches of the arcades provide a sheltered corridor, and the sense of rhythm created by the regular lines of arch supports is interrupted only by the position of the church at the far end.

The plan of the 48- by 134-meter square (figure 47) shows that three sides are surrounded by the arcade, while the fourth is closed by the concave facade of the Baroque-style church. The church, in fact, generates a sense of embracing intimacy that is the compositional keynote of this square. Actually, only the church facade faces squarely down the axis of the piazza. Viewed from the rear, the building sits somewhat at an angle to the square. The extreme left-hand portion is actually part of another building and the entrance to a small street adjoining the square. From the point of view of the church's interior, the concave facade that cuts the front at an angle is a disadvantage in design. Clearly, the configuration of the square as assserted by the manner in which the facades of the structures surrounded it, even though, as we can deduce from architectural history, the church facade was a later Baroque addition to the arcades on three sides of the square that date from the Renaissance.

The composition of this square is a clear example of the Italian talent for transforming external space into roomlike interior space. Its magnificently patterned pavement completed in 1494 is as carefully designed as if it were flooring fitted in a private living room. In these and other features the Piazza Ducale is a particularly intriguing reflection of Italian perceptions of exterior space.

There are numerous other squares in Italy that demonstrate the close relationship between the enclosure of space and an exterior space formed by concave walls. The main square in front of St. Peter's Church in Rome is embraced by semicircular arcades, and the Piazza del Mercato in Lucca has an elliptical shape formed by the buildings that line it. Walls that curve inward impart to external space centripetal and convergent qualities and serve to heighten its impact. Curved walls about an external space also facilitate the figure-forming qualities of the Gestalt "law of the inside," in clear contrast to the vague, centrifugal tendencies of natural space.

With relation to this effect, let us examine the qualities of the square that result from the presence of inside corners. In a simple box inside corners are formed where the sides meet on the interior of the box, and outside corners where the sides meet on the exterior (figure 48). Outside corners are of course created easily in external space but not inside corners because of the relationship of buildings to streets. The very character of the grid system of streets ensures that all the inside corners are disrupted (figure 49a). An example of a large external space without corners is Washington Square in New York City (figure 49c). As many as fourteen streets converge on this square, robbing it of all its potential inside corners and providing a sharp contrast to the external spaces of European cities where genuine inside corners are numerous (figure 48b).

Yet external space without corners is qualitatively inferior to that enclosed by well-defined inside corners. It is not easy to explain why, except that a feeling of intimacy and security is much more likely in squares with inside corners uninterrupted by converging streets. This is demonstrated in the drawings in figure 50. In the case where four round pillars are set up, as in drawing (a), the space resulting from their interaction provides almost no sense of enclosure, since round pillars by

44
Negative and positive
prints of Giambattista
Nolli's map of Rome,
1748

45
Positive and negative prints of an old map of Edo (Tokyo)
(Source: *Kohan Edo-zu Shūsei* [*A Collection of Old Edo Maps*], vol. 7)

46
Piazza Ducale, Vigevano,
Italy
(Photograph: Yoshinobu
Ashihara)

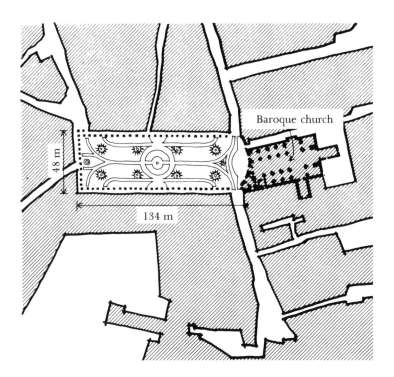

47
Piazza Ducale, Vigevano,
Italy

nature do not indicate direction. If instead four walls are put up, as in drawing (b), their mutual interposition forms a kind of enclosed space, but it lacks definition and clarity because the corners are open. When, finally, angled walls are set up at four corners, as in drawing (c), a mutually reinforcing sense of enclosure is created.[10]

Here the "law of enclosure" or the "law of the inside," as described by Wolfgang Metzger in *Gesetze des Sehens*, is applicable. In other words, areas that are clearly outlined so that they are partially or completely encircled emerge more easily as integrated figures. A square becomes a clearly defined enclosed territory by virtue of its inside corners. As a river slows and eddies in an inlet, in these corners people tend to pause and linger and eventually to put out chairs and sit down to relax. In European cities spaces that preserve the integrity of the corner are an important attraction, invariably embracing the visitor. When buildings are built along streets laid out in a grid pattern, all the corners become outside corners, cold, callous spaces of the city that seem to repulse, rather than to invite, people whereas inside corners draw people into a warm and coherent city space.

A modern-day external space that demonstrates the effective use of inside corners formed by surrounding architecture is the sunken garden. This type of design came into practice only in the twentieth century. It is essentially a hollowed-out courtyard. New York's Rockefeller Center Plaza was a forerunner in sunken garden design, and it is now recognized as one of the most successful examples of this design. It is a landmark no visitor to the city can afford to miss. The most significant feature of Rockefeller

48
Inside and outside corners of a traditional Japanese measuring cup (*masu*)

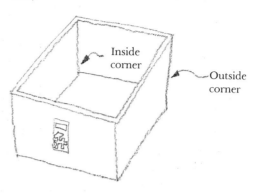

Inside corner

Outside corner

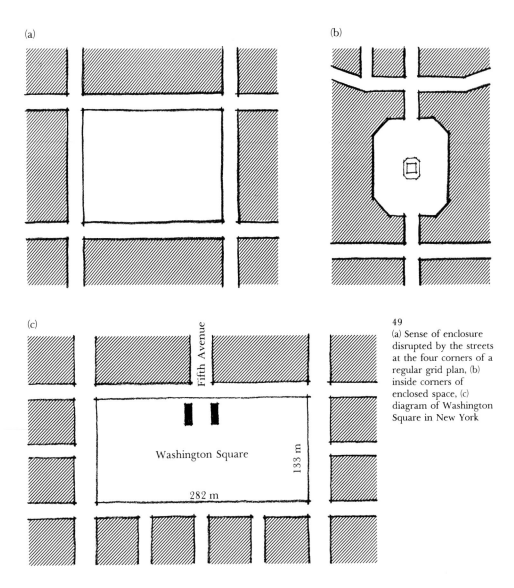

(a)

(b)

(c)

Fifth Avenue

Washington Square

133 m

282 m

49
(a) Sense of enclosure disrupted by the streets at the four corners of a regular grid plan, (b) inside corners of enclosed space, (c) diagram of Washington Square in New York

Center is the lowered area before the RCA building, where an enclosed space is created. Within it one portion has been lowered even further to form the Lower Plaza (raising it would have formed outside corners); the lowering of this portion creates four solid inside corners that foster the Gestalt quality of figure, producing in exterior space the sensation of being "inside." This unique sunken garden creates a closely integrated space using the side walls of the garden to form inside corners just as the walls of adjacent buildings formed the enclosure of an Italian piazza.

By 1960 several high-rise buildings constituting the new Rockefeller Center had been built along Sixth Avenue on the west side, each with its own public open space at street level, but the D/H proportions of these designs are generally inferior to those of the original sunken garden at Rockefeller Center. As Bernard Spring has observed, no subsequent design has yet appeared that can equal this famous precedent constructed well before World War II.[11] A twentieth-century example of neo-Baroque-style symmetry, the plaza is now a major exterior space in New York inseparable from the life of the city.

Because of the difficulty of creating spaces with inside corners in cities where the arrangement of streets is already established, sunken gardens have come to be used in urban design to create exterior spaces rich in Gestalt qualities. Today there are some examples in Tokyo as well: one is in Uchisaiwai-cho, a specially designated area for new urban development near Ginza (figure 51), and the other is part of the Dai-ichi Kangyō Bank head office building in Hibiya (figures 52, 53, and 54). Both are built at the foot of

(a)

(b)

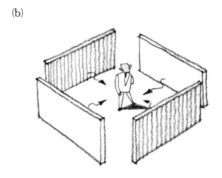

(c)

50
Degrees of enclosure

51
Model of sunken garden
in Uchisaiwai-cho,
Tokyo

52
Sunken garden in the
Dai-ichi Kangyō Bank
building
(Photograph: Akio
Kawasumi)

53
Portion of sunken
garden of Dai-ichi
Kangyō Bank building
(Photograph: Akio
Kawasumi)

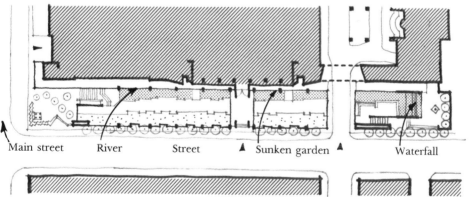

Main street   River   Street   ▲ Sunken garden ▲   Waterfall

54
Plan of Dai-ichi Kangyō
Bank sunken garden

high-rise office buildings. The Dai-ichi
Kangyō Bank's sunken garden contains a
waterfall and a stream accentuated with
ceramic shapes of various colors. This is
my own design, combining ideas I have
hoped to realize in actual buildings for a
long time.

3

External Appearance in Architecture

Elements of External Appearance

The boundary line that divides interior and exterior in architecture is vital, for it determines not only the external character of a building but the townscape about it as well. There was a time when streets in Europe and Japan were lined with rather similar types of buildings, and so townscapes were somewhat homogeneous. In the masonry construction of Europe, stone or brick from the local area was commonly used (figure 55). In Japan, all buildings were of wood, using cedar or cypress for structural members and local clay for roof tiles (figure 56).

Built within the limits of contemporary architectural know-how, and with the distinctive materials of the locality, the houses that made up the townscape of the traditional city were of much the same composition and character. Today highly unified townscapes may still be found in southern Italy and the Greek islands, where all the houses are customarily whitewashed, a practice that imparts a sense of continuity to the townscape, and the white of the townscape stands out in sharp contrast to the dull hues of the surrounding landscape.

In this century, with the advent of modern architecture, townscapes have undergone radical changes as the function and scale of buildings multiplied. In contrast to the traditional pattern whereby buildings consistently faced directly on the streets, various innovations in the use of space, including the generous spacing of high-rise structures, have been adopted. Building materials, no longer limited by what is locally available, now include versatile and colorful industrial products (figure 57). Glass, metal panel, ceramic tile, and concrete facades mix and mingle in unruly profusion along the

55
Townscape of masonry
architecture, Europe
(Photograph: Yoshinobu
Ashihara)

56
Townscape of wooden
architecture, Japan
(Photograph: Yoshinobu
Ashihara

57
Heterogeneous
townscape in modern
cities
(Photograph: Yoshinobu
Ashihara)

58
Glass facade of Fuji Film
building, Yoshinobu
Ashihara, architect.
(Photograph: Masao
Arai)

streets. The rule of exterior homogeneity that provided the basic principle of the aesthetic townscape in the past has been superseded. For the modern, composite townscape made up of heterogeneous structures a new set of aesthetic rules is essential. So far, no theory has been advanced that can provide strong defining principles for such townscapes. In any case, before any theory is possible, we need to know more about the effects of certain exterior building materials. Glass and metal are two materials that are so important today that is often said they actually made modern architecture possible. Here, I would like to examine the relation of modern building materials to the exterior appearance of architecture.

The results of an analysis of the proportion of exterior wall surface to window surface in major modern high-rise buildings in New York and Tokyo are given in table 1. In buildings like the NHK Broadcasting Center or the head office building of the Fuji Film Company (figure 58), where glass covers not only the window panes but also the spandrels, the total glass surface area amounts to more than 70 percent, so that by day the buildings appear to be almost entirely covered with glass. At night, however, because the spandrels are dark, not illuminated like the windows, the building takes on a very different appearance.

Another factor that determines the proportion of glass area visible is the angle of vision. If the window sashes protrude some distance beyond the glass (figure 59), the glass is hidden by the sashes when viewed at an angle, and only the protruding metal is visible. In buildings where the sashes protrude only slightly beyond the glass surface, a large amount of glass is visible even from the side. The

Table 1
Percentages of different building materials used on the exterior

	Stone, tile, PC concrete	Glass	Metal panel	Window sashes
Tokyo				
Tokyo Kaijo building	57.9	35.6		6.5
Kasumigaseki building		33.3	56.3	10.4
IBM Japan building	63.3	36.5		0.2
Fuji Film Head Office building	8.6	73.0		15.6
NHK Broadcasting Center		80.6		19.4
Shinjuku Mitsui building		52.1	29.7	18.2
Shinjuku Sumitomo building		19.1	77.9	3.0
International Communication Center		15.5	82.7	1.8
New York				
Seagram building		57.8	22.1	20.1
Chase Manhattan building		50.0	44.5	5.1

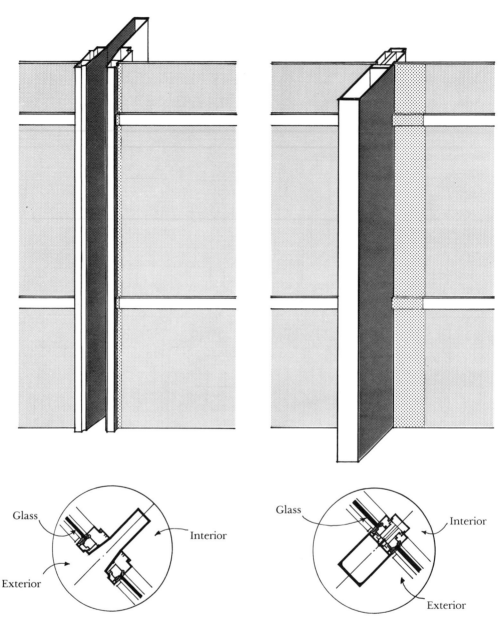

Glass

Interior

Exterior

Glass

Interior

Exterior

59
Building facades with
recessed and protruding
sashes

section plan for sashes may be determined by considerations such as tensile strength and wind pressure, but the extent to which they protrude beyond the glass surface is up to the experience and skill of the architect. Sash treatment is an important element in design, for it determines the overall effect of high-rise buildings, which are most often viewed from below. If the windows are deeply recessed or if there are verandas or other overhangs, the window surfaces are largely obscured. By day such a building looks like a deeply incised sculpture, but at night, because, as in medieval architecture, the quantity of light it transmits is low, it loses much of this modern character.

In these ways, the external appearance of individual buildings is extremely important to the entire townscape. Architects must be aware of how the building materials will appear close up, how the vertical articulation of the facade will be affected by the extent to which the framework of window sashes protrudes when viewed at an intermediate distance, and how protruding eaves or verandas will affect the horizontal articulation.[1] Vertical and horizontal articulation are design considerations related solely to the surface appearance of a building. Recent architecture reflects efforts to depart from the simple glass boxes so common among the early high-rise buildings of the modern style and to give building exteriors expression based on interior functions. One example is the UN building in New York, where the floors reserved for the building's mechanical plant are signaled by the absence of windows at three levels. Another is the Dai-ichi Kangyō Bank building in Tokyo where the intake and exhaust vents for air-conditioning are deliberately exposed (figure 60). The "twin

tower" concept featuring two low buildings placed side by side in place of one larger high-rise structure and the use of diagonal roof lines such as New York's Citicorp Center are other design innovations.

In the Dai-ichi Kangyō Bank building I experimented with a combination of granite (Portuguese granite embedded in precast concrete and finished with a flame-chipped texture) and glass on the exterior (figure 61). The exhaust and emergency smoke outlets are cut back deeply on every floor, producing a vertical "zipper-tooth" effect on the building exterior. Protruding window sashes, as in the Seagram building in New York, provide for the vertical articulation of the design.

Primary and Secondary Profiles

In contrast to Italy and Greece, Japanese shopping streets are filled with a plethora of perpendicular signboards and other fixtures that project over the building facades, so that a town's skyline is not defined by the buildings' roofs but by the collective clutter of these fixtures. Since they are often temporary, many are light enough to flap in the wind, contributing very little to a solid, clear profile for the townscape. The streets are often aflutter with banners advertising bargain sales, current movies, or newly released records mixed in with plastic cherry blossoms or artificial autumn leaves dangling from shops to lend a feeling of festivity to spring and autumn sales (figure 62). Shopfronts are crowded with a lively miscellany of temporary bargain stalls, billboards, banners, and other ephemera. There are fancy hanging street lamps and a profusion of electric lines and advertisements attached to utility poles. Perpendicular signboards cling to buildings almost

60
Variety of expressions in
high-rise buildings

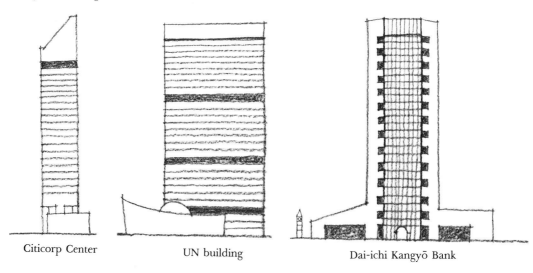

Citicorp Center   UN building   Dai-ichi Kangyō Bank

61
Dai-ichi Kangyō Bank
building, Tokyo
(Photograph: Hisaaki
Suehiro)

62
Ephemera in the
secondary profile of a
shopping street in Japan
(Photograph: Sumiho
Ōta)

from top to bottom in overlapping multiplicity, and the traffic signs, which ought to be both functional and easy to see, are often posted in unsightly and tedious repetition.

It can be mathematically calculated that if, for example, a signboard protrudes 1 meter from a building (the maximum width permitted by building codes), 2 meters of the building wall will not be visible at an angle of 27 degrees (tan 27° = 2), 3 meters at an angle of 18 degrees, and none from a position parallel to the signboard. This means that the narrower the street, the more likely it is that protruding signboards will obscure the fronts of the buildings. In Japan perpendicular signboards are now the norm, and they are so numerous that the front walls of buildings are often almost completely obscured and can contribute little to the definition of the townscape.

Let us call the outline of a building's front exterior its "primary profile" and that created by the protruding or temporary ephemera attached to it the "secondary profile."[2] In general, European townscapes are defined by the primary profile, while Asian—think of Hong Kong, as well as cities in both Korea and Japan—are characteristically dominated by the secondary profile.

In Italian cities the streets have Gestalt qualities as figures with relation to the exterior walls of buildings whose presence dominates them. In the shopping districts of Japanese cities, however, far from helping to define the street as figure, the walls, obscured by loose, fluttering banners, and protruding miscellany, blur the outline of the primary profile. Japanese painters often become skillful at painting European landscapes but find it extremely difficult to capture the Japanese townscape on canvas. This is not altogether surprising, for the primary profile that defines European townscapes presents a clear, orderly architecture that is easy to paint, not at all the disarray of the unstructured secondary profile that dominates the Japanese townscape.

Recently some Japanese buildings have begun to adopt signboards of uniform size and have lined them up evenly in an attempt at some unified design effect. Signboards in an orderly or rhythmic arrangement can be incorporated into the primary profile of buildings (figure 63). If tastefully designed, they can in fact improve the profile of a townscape.

In the islands of the Aegean Sea and in southern Italy, the outlines of the townscapes are not consistently defined, yet a certain order prevails which makes them attractive subjects for painting. These towns derive their artistic appeal, despite the seeming disarray of architectural outlines, from the assertiveness of the primary profile. Many other mature townscapes in Europe demonstrate that the less there is of a secondary profile, the more refined the townscape. There is something to be said, nonetheless, for the spontaneous, heterogeneous townscape that typifies Asian cities. In a later chapter I shall explore in greater detail the unique qualities that give these streets their exotic character.

The quality of a townscape also depends on the visibility of the buildings. If, on a street lined on both sides with buildings, the viewpoint is set at a position parallel to the building and very close to that line, theoretically none of the building wall will enter the field of vision. Only the protruding fixtures of the secondary profile may be visible. As a person moves farther away from the edge of

63
Uniform array of
signboards
(Photograph: Yoshinobu
Ashihara)

the street, the faces of buildings enter the field of vision, and the area of the visible building facade increases. Meanwhile the area of the secondary profile does not change appreciably, but the farther one moves away, the greater the amount of wall area that is visible. In other words, the farther into the street one stands, the more of the actual facade of the building emerges and the smaller the portion obscured by secondary profile elements. Then, from a spot directly in front of a building, the entire front enters the field of vision, and the side walls recede from view. The hanging street signs and other protrusions are not visible, save for their width, and the secondary profile gives way at last to the primary in the field of vision. Such a frontal perspective of a building, needless to say, creates the strongest impression and contributes most richly to a townscape.

Frontality figures significantly in the formation of the primary profile. Starting in the Renaissance, cities in Europe were planned in such a way that buildings could be viewed from the front and at a distance two to three times their height (D/H = 2 or 3). Architecture was designed with regard to the impact of its frontality on the townscape, a characteristic seen over and over again in the squares of Europe. The streets of Paris are ingeniously laid out to pivot at some historical building or monument, which in turn commands grand vistas of the surrounding area. This, of course, owes its concept to the French Baroque mind. If, as advocated by Le Corbusier, Paris had been rebuilt in clusters of skyscrapers scattered over broad spaces, there would be a quite different townscape.

Turning to look at the Japanese landscape, it is clear that frontality, save in the layout of temples within their compounds, was precluded by constraints of space. City blocks are irregularly divided and the fronts of buildings crop up in the most unexpected places. The chance view of a portion of the front of one building beyond many others is quite different from the undisturbed frontality of a building designed to be seen schematically from top to bottom. The difference in effect may be grasped by comparing the Tokyo Tower, crouched in a crowded downtown area, to the Eiffel Tower, ensconced over the wide avenues of central Paris.

A well-known townscape in Japan is Tokyo's Ginza Avenue. Taking a close look at its composition, we will examine the number of protruding signboards hanging in the 900 meter portion of this street between the first and eighth blocks. Since the signboards are placed one above another in vertical rows, the actual effect is best gauged by counting these rows rather than each individual signboard. The letter N stands for the number of rows of signboards.

Calculated in this fashion, as shown in tables 2 and 3, we find that there are 199 rows of perpendicular signboards on both sides of Ginza Avenue. The total surface area occupied by the signboards (A) adds up to 1,523 square meters, and, given the length of the street under consideration (L), A/L = 0.84 m^2, meaning that for every meter of the street, there are 0.84 square meters of signboard. Thus L/N = 9.1 meters, meaning, as shown in the table, that one encounters a perpendicular signboard at an average of every 9.1 meters along the street. Applying these figures roughly, and hypothesizing that every 10 meters or so there is a signboard jutting out a meter from the building, we can construct a graph such as

Table 2
Survey of signboards on Ginza Avenue (August 1978)

Location	Total length of street in meters (L)	Total surface area of signboards in square meters (A)	Number of signboards (N)	A/L m^2	L/N m
Ginza 1 to 8 *chome* (west side)	901	960	111	1.07	8.12
Ginza 1 to 8 *chome* (east side)	910	563	88	0.62	10.34
Ginza 1 to 8 *chome* (both sides)	1,811	1,523	199	0.84	9.10

Note: "*Chome*" corresponds to a city block, the basic unit of the city.

Table 3
Sectional Survey of signboards on Ginza Avenue (August 1978)

Location along Ginza Avenue	Length of street section in meters (L)	Total surface area of signboards in square meters (A)	Number of vertical rows of signboards (N)	A/L m^2	L/N m
1 *chome*					
West side	111	92	11	0.83	10.09
East side	126	115	22	0.91	5.73
2 *chome*					
West side	111	153	17	1.38	6.53
East side	111	104	8	0.94	13.88
3 *chome*					
West side	119	132	12	1.11	9.92
East side	119	26	2	0.22	59.50
4 *chome*					
West side	94	79	7	0.84	13.43
East side	94	55	12	0.59	7.83
5 *chome*					
West side	108	101	6	0.94	18.00
East side	108	50	7	0.46	15.43
6 *chome*					
West side	113	169	21	1.50	5.38
East side	113	50	6	0.44	18.83
7 *chome*					
West side	114	101	20	0.89	5.70
East side	114	59	16	0.52	7.13
8 *chome*					
West side	131	133	17	1.02	7.71
East side	125	104	15	0.83	8.33

Note: "*Chome*" corresponds to a city block, the basic unit of the city.

shown in figure 64. By referring to this graph and the photographs in figure 65, we can see that, at a distance of about 3 meters from the side of the street, the walls of the buildings that form the primary profile are almost invisible. At about 6 meters away the space obscured by the signboards and the area of the actual facades of the buildings are about equal. The farther away one stands, the more surface area of the primary profile comes into view. Thus, if the sidewalks are not at least 3 meters wide, the impression of the townscape will be quite vague.

To improve the appearance of the downtown areas of Japanese cities, the primary profiles of the buildings must be clarified and the secondary profiles decreased as much as possible so that the townscape will make a bolder impression and have a more distinctive character. The main thoroughfares at the center of the city should be made as wide as possible. The typical main street in Tokyo is now less than 30 meters wide, while, for example, the Champs-Élysées in Paris is approximately 70 meters wide. As we demonstrated earlier, the wider the street, the greater will be the visible portion of the primary profile of the buildings. For the same reason, the sidewalks should be at the very least 3 meters wide, or wider if possible. In the case of Ginza Avenue the sidewalks are unusually wide for Japan at 6.5 meters. By comparison, the sidewalks of the Champs-Élysées are fully 11.5 meters wide (figure 66). The spatial experience possible at the outermost limit of a wide sidewalk is like that felt when standing in the middle of the street in a scramble intersection or when the streets are blocked off to traffic. Benches, drinking fountains, sculptures, public telephones, clocks, street lamps, information

boards, and other fixtures should be carefully harmonized on these broad sidewalks to make the street function not only as a space for traffic but as the scene of human interaction and activity.

Finally, the secondary profile that obstructs the primary profile of the buildings should be strictly limited, especially in the case of perpendicular hanging signboards. Variety and Gestalt effects can be obtained by creating "inside corners" and sunken gardens. The "imageability" of the townscape can be augmented by applying the principles of frontality and immediacy.

I have, of course, been describing the townscapes of major streets. There is naturally a very different atmosphere to be found in the old sections of European cities, or in the back streets of shopping areas of Japanese towns, where the townscape is brought down to a human scale notably by narrow streets and lower buildings. Japan's small shopping streets are alight with neon signs and colorful advertising (figure 67), some consisting only of a secondary profile. Here the lively, crowded atmosphere gives this kind of townscape a certain fascination and appeal.

The Nightscape and Figure-Ground Reversal

While living in New York I became aware of the significance of the urban nightscape. Often in the evening after work I would watch from the single window of my tiny Manhattan apartment the innumerable windows of high-rise apartment buildings across the city light up. As darkness fell, the walls of the buildings would recede into the night, until all that remained was the bright glow of windows, a totally different configuration than in the daytime. This experience led me to

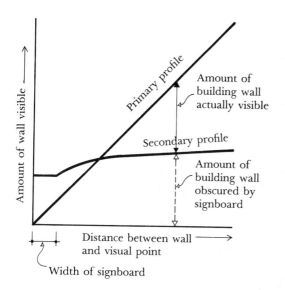

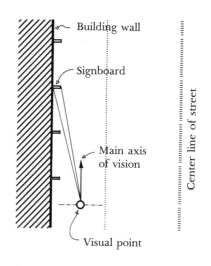

Primary profile

Amount of building wall actually visible

Secondary profile

Amount of building wall obscured by signboard

Amount of wall visible

Distance between wall and visual point

Width of signboard

Building wall

Signboard

Main axis of vision

Visual point

Center line of street

Plan of street

64
Appearance of primary
and secondary profiles

65
Primary and secondary
profiles of Ginza Avenue
(Photograph: Yoshinobu
Ashihara)

(a)

(b)

Viewing at a point 3 m away
from the west side of the street

6 m away from the west side

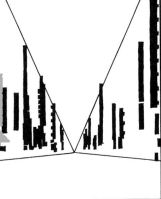
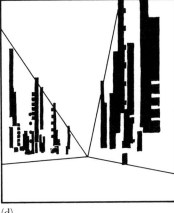
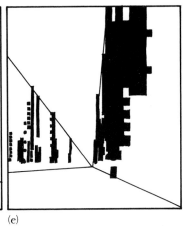

·nter

(d)
6 m away from the east side

(e)
3 m away from the east side

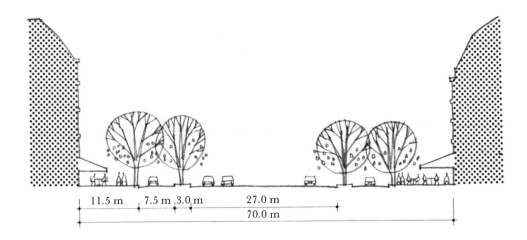

11.5 m   7.5 m 3.0 m   27.0 m

70.0 m

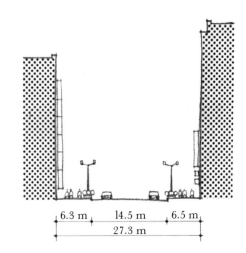

66
Cross-section diagrams
of Champs-Élysées
(above) and Ginza
Avenue (below)

6.3 m   14.5 m   6.5 m

27.3 m

67
Back streets of a
Japanese city
(Photograph: Sumiho
Ōta)

consider the nightscape in the external
design of architecture.

During daylight hours the character of
a townscape is determined by the exterior
walls of buildings; windows and other apertures are but a shadowy presence of re-
flecting glass. Yet, once night falls, walls
withdraw from view and the windows
take over center stage, producing in effect
a figure-ground reversal (figure 68). Since
inside is brighter than outside, the interior space that could not be seen by day
becomes visible, and as buildings begin to
transmit light, their interior spaces suddenly appear to draw nearer, disclosing
activities that in the daytime were totally
hidden. To me, these tiny, distant windows, their illumination reaching out into
the night, seem to symbolize a sense of
communion among people, the longing
for the intimacy of the small community.
From faraway, the city nightscape merges
with the starlit sky. Like the windows
glowing against the darkened city, the
stars in the night sky become figures in
the Gestalt sense. We often imagine that
there are living beings in stars, and this is
closely associated with the presence of
human activity the illuminated windows
of a nightscape represent.

Let us consider for a moment the differences between architecture by day and
by night. By day architecture is viewed in
reflected light, and by night it is illuminated by light transmitted from within.
Historically, the exterior parts of buildings
have been designed to be viewed in reflected light. In fact, it is safe to say that
until modern times no buildings were
built with their appearance at night a
prime consideration. One may, upon a
moonlit night, climb the Acropolis to enjoy the silhouette of the Parthenon's
majestic columns against a moonlit sky,
or gaze at the stars through the arches of

the aqueducts at Nimes or of the Colos-
seum in Rome. But, as a rule, the daytime virtues of architectural masterpieces,
be they Gothic, Renaissance, or Baroque,
are plunged into oblivion at night. If anything of their grandeur remains visible, it
is a looming silhouette. Monolithic brick
or stone architecture was designed to be
seen by day; and, since masonry walls
have relatively few apertures, they release
very little transmitted light. They revert,
at night, to little more than shadowy
agglomerations of stone.

Architecture designed with the nightscape in mind began to develop only
when structures were created that permitted light within to be easily transmitted
outside. Modern architecture broke away
from the constraints of masonry construction, and its large quantities of glass made
possible the reversal of Gestalt figures
represented by a building's walls in the
daytime and by the illuminated windows
at night. In this sense glass is the crucial
material in modern architecture, for it
permits an entirely new perceptual experience that was quite impossible in medieval stone architecture (figure 69).

To gather data on the nightscapes of
buildings, my students at the University
of Tokyo and I conducted a series of observations of the high-rise buildings in
Tokyo's Shinjuku area (figure 70). After
first plotting points at distances in 100
meter intervals in a straight line away
from the buildings, we recorded how the
building appeared at distances of 100
meters, 200 meters, and so on. At 100
meters we found that the angle of elevation when viewing the upper part of the
buildings is over 45 degrees. The fluores-
cent light fixtures on the ceilings of the
rooms inside remain clearly visible so that
the windows themselves do not present a

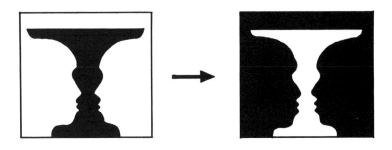

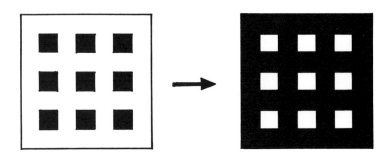

68
Figure-ground reversal
in Edgar Rubin's vase-
faces figure and day and
nighttime townscapes

69
Nightscape of New York
City
(Photograph: Nobutaka
Ashihara)

70
Nightscape of high-rise
buildings in Tokyo's
Shinjuku area
(Photograph: Sumiho
Ōta)

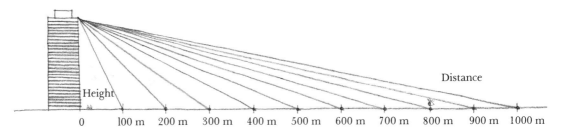

Height

Distance

0   100 m   200 m   300 m   400 m   500 m   600 m   700 m   800 m   900 m   1000 m

71
Observing a high-rise
building at 100 meter
intervals

single integrated form. It is only at a distance of 500 meters that the fixtures become hardly noticeable. Finally, at 800 meters, most observers perceived the lighted windows as discrete Gestalt figures. We thus confirmed that the reversal of figure and ground takes effect at about 800 meters (figures 71 and 72). Naturally, it may be necessary to take into account factors such as climatic conditions and individual differences in eyesight as well as the methods used in the survey. Although rather rudimentary, this study has proved very useful in our own designs. Knowing how a building will appear at night from a given distance makes it possible to design architecture that is attractive both night and day.

Moving even farther away than the 800 meters at which individual buildings present a coherent nightscape, it is possible to appreciate the nightscape of a city as a whole. New York's Manhattan as viewed from Brooklyn Heights is an outstanding example of such a nightscape.

Among contemporary buildings perhaps one of the most beautiful, when viewed at night, is the Seagram building on New York's Park Avenue. The work of Mies van der Rohe, its window sashes are made entirely of bronze, and the glass has a pale bronze color. Mies must have given careful thought to the effect of the illumination from the windows at night. The building's nightscape has such unity that the total Gestalt quality of the building would suffer if just one window were blacked out. The proportion of glass in the Seagram building is 57.8 percent, over half the surface area, and this vastly increases the amount of light transmitted by the building facade.

The most effective way to enhance the nighttime beauty of a building is to set the glass flush with the outer wall. The

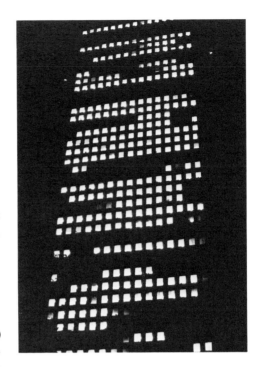

72
Reversal of figure and ground at night
(Photograph: Sumiho Ōta)

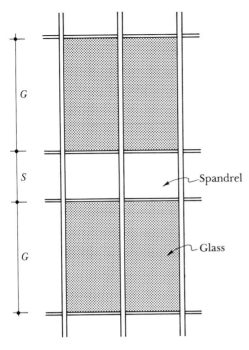

G

S

Spandrel

G

Glass

73
Comparison of height of
glass and spandrel
surfaces

ideal for architecture designed for day-time is for glassed-in areas to be recessed in a building facade, or for verandas or other protrusions to be added so that the building surfaces are thrown into relief by the overhead sunlight. At night, when veiwed from below, the window sill and eaves block out the illuminated glass, and the building's contribution to the night-scape is much reduced.

The appearance of a building at night is also affected by the height of glass por-tions (*G*) in relation to the height of the spandrels in between (*S*). As Mies demon-strated in the Seagram building, it is im-portant to achieve a proportion of *G/S* greater than 1 (figure 73). New York mod-ern dancer Marilyn Wood showed a clear appreciation of the superb effect of the unobstructed vertical plane in the Sea-gram building when she staged an eve-ning performance in the illuminated windows of the building (figure 74).

The Tokyo Metropolitan Government building (Kenzō Tange, architect) is like-wise of metal and glass but has verandas protruding from the facade. In the day-time it exhibits the best qualities of tradi-tional Japanese architecture with its deeply recessed eaves, but at night it withdraws and would never be suitable as a stage for such a performance of dancers (figures 75a and b). At least for myself, the sight of the Seagram building is far more beautiful and fantastic lit up at night than in the daytime, and it leaves a more lasting impression. The Tokyo Metropolitan Government building, on the other hand, is less memorable at night; it is at its best on a bright, sunny day when deep shadows are cast by the sun overhead.

Buildings with a proportionately small amount of glass on the exterior can be

74
Dancers in night festival
at the Seagram building,
New York
(Photograph: Courtesy of
Marilyn Wood)

75
Tokyo Metropolitan
Government building in
the daytime and at
night
(Photograph Sumiho
Ōta)

made attractive at night by outdoor illumination, as is often used for memorial structures. This kind of lighting does not allow for the figure-ground reversal effect. But another effect can be obtained such as in my design for the Sony building in the Ginza area of Tokyo where interior light reflected by the building's latticed exterior creates a semitranslucent effect (figure 76). Those vertical louvers are made as slender as possible on the exterior side and have specially designed concave surfaces (figure 77) that transmit light. The light reflected off the louvers mingles with that transmitted from inside, as in a Japanese lantern. Even though this building has not been fully lighted in recent years because of the need to conserve energy, it has a distinctive nighttime presence in the area.

One cannot talk about nightscapes of cities without mentioning neon signs. The number of these signs in Japan's cities is perhaps only surpassed by New York's Times Square and Las Vegas. Rooftop or hanging signboards and neon advertising signs are a mixed blessing for the city townscape. Buildings are, of course, designed as complete entities, and an architect goes to great pains to balance the proportions of a building's exterior walls with the size of the utility tower atop it. It is somehow tragic, then, when that carefully designed tower is swathed with gigantic neon advertising signs. It seems as aesthetically misguided as crowning a beautiful woman with an outlandish hat. Hanging signboards and bargain sale banners only add insult to injury, like covering her face with Band-Aids and adhesive tape. At night the building itself withdraws, leaving the neon signs on the rooftop to take over center stage in taudry glory. To continue the metaphor, it is like taking away the beautiful woman

76
Nightscape of Sony
building, Ginza, Tokyo,
Yoshinobu Ashihara,
architect
(Photograph: Masao
Arai)

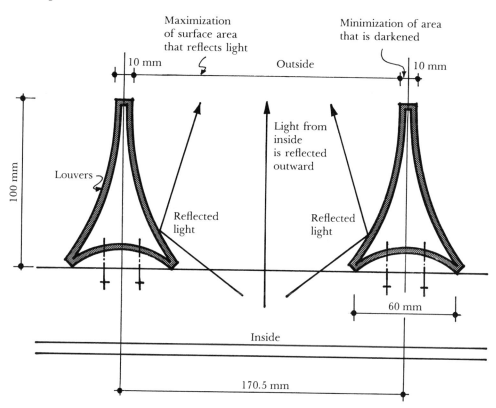

Maximization
of surface area
that reflects light

Minimization of area
that is darkened

10 mm

Outside

10 mm

100 mm

Louvers

Light from
inside
is reflected
outward

Reflected
light

Reflected
light

60 mm

Inside

170.5 mm

78
Daytime and nighttime
in the same townscape,
Shinjuku, Tokyo
(Photograph: Sumiho
Ōta)

and showing off nothing but the preposterous hat. In the daytime no matter how outstanding the design and color of a neon sign, it may be unendurably ugly when viewed together with the building, but at night when only the sign is visible the effect can be pleasing. Depending on how neon signs are arranged, the nightscape can be quite attractive (figure 78a and b).

Visitors to Japan are often overwhelmed and impressed by the energy spent on neon signs in large cities. Yet this cannot really be viewed as a positive, aesthetic aspect of the Japanese townscape. In commercial sections of city centers where the lighting they create at night is very important, neon signs may be permissible in certain prescribed areas as long as they are harmoniously arranged. Outside the city center, however, primary consideration should be accorded the daytime townscape. In either case the use of rooftops of office buildings and condominiums along major streets for rooftop advertising must be combated as this detracts from an aesthetically pleasing townscape. Architects who design buildings for central city areas can help by giving careful attention to both the daytime and nighttime presence of a building in the townscape.

4

Some
Reflections
on Space

Bird's-Eye Views and Curvilinear Landscapes

One of the charms of a city landscape is its overlooks and the opportunities they provide for panoramic views. An overlook allows the eye to grasp the entire territory swiftly and accurately, and in the city, it helps establish familiarity between the viewer and the townscape (figure 79).

The sweeping panorama of Paris, the Eiffel Tower in the distance, that can be viewed from the top of Montmartre facing away from the Sacré-Coeur church is well known. For many a visitor this sight inspires the exhilarating feeling that he has at last seen Paris in its entirety. Rome, too, is famous for its seven hills, from which vantage points overlooking the domed roofs of churches across the city one learns the real meaning of the old adage that "Rome wasn't built in a day."

Among Japan's major cities, Tokyo and Osaka unfortunately have no good vantage points that offer bird's-eye views of the surrounding landscape. Some port cities, such as Kobe and Yokohama, are built on hills that command broad coastal vistas, and these invariably evoke nostalgic and sentimental associations for those who visit. Significantly, it is the wealthy who reside on the upper slopes of the hills in such cities, while the dwellings of ordinary people crowd the lower areas, testifying to the high value attached to the privilege of being able to look down upon the surrounding landscape. Hong Kong is a typical example of such a city.

Looking down and looking up are physiologically quite different, a consideration that should not be overlooked in studying the aesthetic qualities of the townscape. In his research on visual perception, Henry Dreyfuss measured the

79
A view overlooking the
landscape

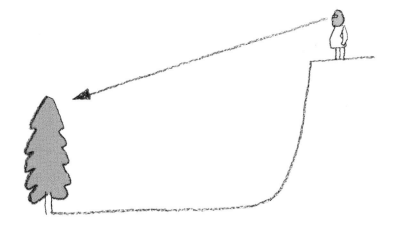

highest, lowest, and optimal angles of fields of vision from an airplane cockpit, using a sample of 1,400 air force cadets. His findings showed that, in general, the angle of depression for a person standing is 10 degrees and for a person sitting 15 degrees. The upper boundary of the field of vision is 50 to 55 degrees, and the lower is 70 to 80 degrees.[1] This is more scientific than Hans Märtens's thesis that the field of vision is a cone of an angle 60 degrees, and it confirms that it is physiologically more natural for man to look down than to look up.[2]

A scholar of townscape theory, Tadahiko Higuchi, has made a valuable study of bird's-eye perspective. In a survey conducted at the Tokyo Tower, he found that persons standing at both the 150- and 250-meter lookout points felt an angle of from 8 to 10 degrees to be the most comfortable.[3] Higuchi's analysis parallels that of Henry Dreyfuss and provides empirical evidence showing that areas within a 10 degree angle of depression are most easily visible to the human eye.

One exemplary bird's-eye view in Japan is from Mt. Hakodate in the northernmost island of Hokkaido, which provides an unobstructed and unsurpassed view of Hakodate Bay, a landscape particularly impressive at night. Higuchi has analyzed this bird's-eye view, finding that an angle of depression of 10 degrees from the summit of the mountain includes an arc that embraces the city of Hakodate proper as well as the oceanfront and port (figures 80 and 81).

Increasing the possibilities for bird's-eye views and making calculated use of field of vision in a townscape can greatly enhance its charm and attractiveness. Towns like San Francisco and Rio de Janeiro, with slopes, stairs, hills, and high places overlooking their ports, invariably leave lasting impressions on those who live or visit there. Townscape composition, then, should exploit the presence of such overlooks wherever possible.

We have discussed the many ways in which the principles of Gestalt psychology can be applied to architectural space. They can help explain the relationship of inside to outside, the reversal of figure and ground in the nightscape, and the spatial qualities of the sunken garden and inside corner space. Here, I should like to experiment by applying the Gestalt principle yet again in considering the aesthetics of the landscape at the edge of a body of water.

When a body of water extends uninterrupted to the horizon and there is no boundary line circumscribing it, it functions simply as the background—land areas constitute the figure, and the water the ground. On the other hand, if there are islands, points of land, opposing shores, or protruding elements in the water, it does become possible for the water to function as figure just as do the encircled spaces with inside corners of a city.

Now let us look at the effect of a coastline or the curved landscape formed at the edge of the sea or lakeshore. We may observe both convex (figure 82) and concave (figure 83) curves in such landscapes, and the aesthetic appeal of the concave curve may be traced to the Gestalt principles of inside corners and enclosed space, the inside being characterized by the elements of figure. A city on the edge of a body of water is particularly striking because of the juxtaposition of the natural and the man-made. In the case of a concave, curved landscape, the water circumscribed by the shoreline and the man-made landscape of a city or port both

80
Bird's-eye view at night
from Mt. Hakodate
(Photograph: Gakutoshi
Kojima)

81
Area falling within field
of vision at angle of
depression of 10 degrees
from the top of Mt.
Hakodate

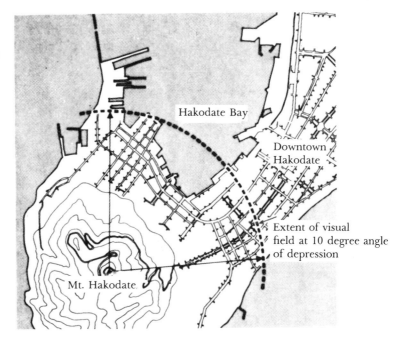

Hakodate Bay

Downtown
Hakodate

Extent of visual
field at 10 degree angle
of depression

Mt. Hakodate

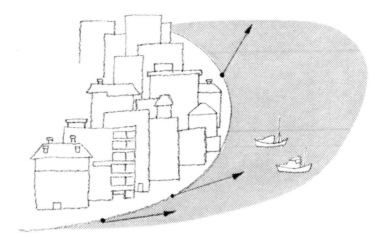

82
Convex curve in seaside
landscape

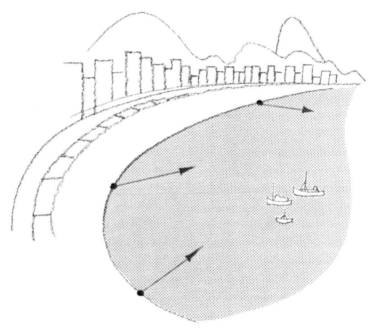

83
Concave curve in
seaside landscape

enter the field of vision, augmenting the aesthetic appeal of the scene. At night a line of street lamps reflected at regular intervals on the water's surface further highlights such a landscape.

In a convex landscape the land juts out into a body of water, and there is no boundary circumscribing the water that surrounds it, so the line of vision is continually directed outward, diminishing the sense of intermingled natural and manmade landscapes. A concave curve calls attention to the body of water, forming a relationship between water and land that is conducive to the reversal of figure and ground, as observed in Edgar Rubin's vase-faces figure, which is much more distinctive and memorable. The Copacabanna in Rio de Janeiro (figure 84) and the Nice seacoast of France (figure 85) are examples of such concave landscapes.

Moreover, if we consider such curved landscapes from the standpoint of the "view from without" and the "view from within" discussed in chapter 1, we might say that, at least in Japan, the perspective from "within" is preferred. For example, the waterfront of the famous Kamo River in Kyoto is crowded with expensive Japanese-style restaurants, although from afar they look like a jumble of crowded tenements (figure 86). Seated within one of these exclusive establishments, however, where dining is attended by cultivated Kyoto geisha, and gazing at the landscape across the Kamo River, one can enjoy one of the most pleasing night sights in Japan. Still this is a clear contrast with such landscapes in the West, where the view from without may be just as impressive as that from within.

Most seascapes extend unbroken from the water's edge to the horizon, uninterrupted by any distinguishing feature that might draw the eye. A scene punctuated by islands or other features, however, is far more striking. One famous example in Japan is that near Ise Shrine in the Futamigaura bay, where the so-called "Wedded Rocks" stand just off the coast. An immense rice straw cord of the type used in Shinto ritual (shimenawa) is tied around them as a symbol of a bond that goes far back in Japanese mythology (figure 87). This pair of rocks brings the scene into focus and gives a sense of cohesiveness to the seascape. Another example is the large torii or symbolic gate that stands in the inlet beyond Itsukushima Shrine near Hiroshima, originally built in the ninth century. The torii, viewed across the high dance platform of the shrine, serves a valuable function aesthetically by bringing the entire seascape into sharp focus (figure 88).[4] The beauty of the Inland Sea, too, can be explained by the fact that the water is dotted with small islands that endow the landscape with points of interest and variety.

Finland is a country famous for its lakes and forests and blessed with beautiful landscapes. The lakes are unrippled and quiet, and the forests along their shores stand reflected on their silvery surfaces, creating truly exquisite landscapes in the dusk of the white arctic nights. If there were no line to define the boundary of the lakes, they would simply blend in and merge with the dusky sky above, but the surrounding forests provide a demarcating border so that lake and sky achieve the qualities of "figure." Here the forest and its reflection, on the one hand, and the lake and sky, on the other (figures 89 and 90), carry off the figure and ground reversal of the vase-faces diagram.

A landscape that exhibits yet another phenomenon is found in Japan in the

84
Curve of Copacabana
Beach, Rio de Janeiro
(Photograph: Yoshinobu
Ashihara)

85
Curve of seacoast, Nice,
France
(Photograph: Yoshinobu
Ashihara)

86
Restaurants along the
Kamo River, Kyoto
(Photograph: Yoshinobu
Ashihara)

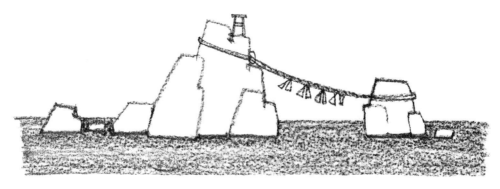

87
Wedded Rocks in
Futamigaura Bay near
Ise

88
Itsukushima Shrine with
torii in the distance,
Miyajima
(Photograph: Yukio
Futagawa)

89
Landscape in the white
night in Finland
(Photograph: Yoshinobu
Ashihara)

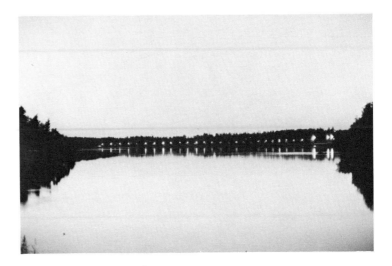

90
Analysis of the
landscape

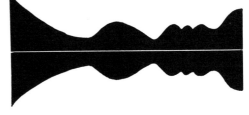

Lake and sky achieve the qualities of "figure."

Edgar Rubin's vase-face diagram can be applied to
the actual landscape.

91
" Bridge over the
heavens" (Ama no
Hashidate) as viewed
from Ōuchi Pass
(Photograph: Yoshinobu
Ashihara)

92
Viewing the landscape
upside down

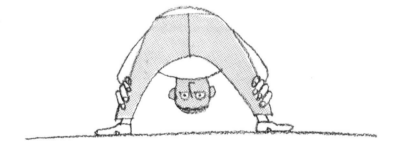

93
The imagination
transports one to small
spaces

Miyazu area north of Kyoto. There, in the Wakasa Bay National Park, a slender, pine-tree-lined cape since the Edo period called the "bridge over the heavens" (Ama no Hashidate), extends across the water (figure 91). If one stands backward from nearby Mt. Nariai or at Ōuchi Pass and gazes out upside down between his legs at this landscape (figure 92), the line of pine trees crossing the bay seems to arch over the sky rather than the water. In this case, while the trees are not re-flected in the water because of the waves, the water and sky appear to have re-versed positions, and there does, in fact, seem to be a bridge over the heavens. This sight has rightfully earned a place among Japan's three most famous land-scapes, and it, too, can be explained in terms of the principles of Gestalt psychology.

In Tokyo Bay and many similar loca-tions around the world, artificial land is being created by landfills jutting out into bodies of water. Today, I believe, we have reached a stage where the civil engi-neers who direct these projects should give careful thought not only to function and efficiency but to aesthetic qualities, and they should strive to incorporate curved landscapes and other features that will improve the appeal of the scenery they are creating.

In Praise of Small Spaces

Gaston Bachelard's insight, that poets are always ready to see the big within the small, bears consideration from the point of view of architecture.[5] Large spaces have merit for qualities that cannot be achieved otherwise, but small spaces also possess inestimable charm. Take anything little—a puppy, a kitten, a tree in *bonsai* miniature, or a small doll—these are all

things that are lovely and appealing because of their diminutive size, like a pearl
sitting in the palm of your hand. Does it
not seem that little things evoke the future? Fantasy? Romance? In contrast to
big things, they beckon one into an imaginary world, a world that promises dis-
covery of something secret and unknown.

Our appreciation of the small is far
from intellectual; it is intuitive, instinctual.
"Platonic dialectics of large and small do
not suffice for us to become cognizant of
the dynamic virtues of miniature thinking.
One must go beyond logic in order to experience what is large in what is small,"
says Bachelard.[6] Suppose, for example,
there is an apple before you on the table.
Childish exercise as it may seem, try to
imagine that you are inside the apple.
Would it not be spacious and open inside? In the mind's eye, it could be a tre-
mendously vast, perhaps tranquil, interior
space. It is the world of the imagination
that brings genuine peace of mind, and a
sense of fulfillment and well-being. Entrance into small spaces requires the imaginative power to reduce oneself to a
fraction of his size, and those who have it
can be transported to the world of cre-
ativity.[7] To imagine yourself a giant, on
the other hand, somehow does not trigger
the fancy; in big things it is difficult to see
the small. In this lies the significance of
"small spaces" (figure 93).

As Bachelard points out, in the world
of a child's imagination it is possible to
enter the mouths of whales or to shrink
down to a size small enough to get into
the stomach of a frog, showing that in the
imaginary world, the small is compatible
with the big. This type of allegory is common in fairy tales around the world and
is unmistakably connected with the sense
of comfort and satisfaction in imagining

oneself inside a creature's body. Psychologically, it might be explained in terms of the Yona complex or the desire to return to the womb. Man carries with him always the subconscious yet sustained memory of the bliss and security of his mother's gentle embrace.

A reappraisal of the small and intimate is needed today as we face the problems of immense cities, dense population, and high technology. Cities have always been valued for the greatly expanded opportunities they provide for people to meet and mingle through the concentration of population. Their attractions lie in convenience, the fast pace of life, and the freedom imparted by anonymity. As industrialization progresses, populations all over the world flood into the cities. Often the emergence of a technologically advanced society has been so sudden that city building cannot keep pace, and uncontrolled urban jungles have sprung up around the globe. Hyperactive growth has produced jumbled cities of mammoth proportions, cities that threaten to go out of man's control and become wastelands of alienation and decadence. Human beings can only suffer from constant noise, jostling crowds, and the clamor of speeding automobiles and trains. The whirl of energy of the city has grown overwhelming, and modern man has developed a kind of allergy to the vast chaos of the city.

In the field of architecture substantial interest has at last begun to focus on small spaces as well as large, a movement that seems to reflect the desire of modern man to recover some of the humane comforts that were once part of city living. The realization is finally emerging that, for people who live in the cities, even urban residential areas must be places of tranquility and comfort, at least partially removed from the bustle and clamor of a city's center.

The city has been described as a hierarchical order starting with individual private homes and extending to the community at large. The more a city expands in size and the more crowded it is, the more indispensable are small, tranquil places. Small does not necessarily mean cramped; it can suggest coziness, intimacy, and friendliness. Japanese tradition has shown that sometimes certain values can only be realized in smallness, as demonstrated by a potted *bonsai* or by the modest tea ceremony house.

Small spaces impart a luxurious sense of seclusion and privacy that can never be experienced in large spaces. They express above all that which is personal and private and are places of tranquility, imagination, poesy, and humanity. These qualitites contrast with the anonymity, noise, inhumaneness, and blinding reality of the crowded city. Just as the sun rises in the east to shine on the myriad activities of the day and sinks to quiet repose in the west at evening, man's daytime business may go on in large, open spaces, but at night he wants to escape to the quiet of small spaces, to the comfort and warmth of his hearth or the meditative quiet of his study.

Another outstanding type of small space, and one of my favorites, is the sauna. I happened upon a superlative one in Finland, a tidy wooden hut among the trees alongside a lake, at that time shimmering in the light of the midnight sun. Inside, a wood fire heated the room to about 100° C, but, because the air was dry, the high temperature was marvelously refreshing. Stones were stacked on a blazing stove, and cold water ladled over them until the room steamed with an ex-cruciating heat. To sit there, enduring the heat as long as possible pouring with sweat, and then, having reached one's limit, to burst forth and plunge into the silvery cool of the lake, is a wonderfully exhilarating experience, especially when repeated a few times.

The sauna hut is a simple, dim, "small space." It can impart the same tranquil feeling that Japanese associate with Zen meditation or the tea ceremony. Close to the simple elements of nature, a real sauna breathes the fragrance of wood. It is a contemplative, intimate place where an individual creates and adjusts an at-mosphere to the needs of his own person until he experiences a sense of peace and fulfillment. It is a space that vanquishes accumulated tensions and bestows replen-ishing energy (figures 94 and 95).

To trace the rediscovery of small spaces in architecture, let us go back to the Modern Architecture Movement that be-gan around the 1920s. Among its slogans was the new notion of buildings as "ma-chines for living in," and many architects were attracted to the principles of city planning advocated by Le Corbusier based on his slogan *"soleil, l'éspace, ver-due."* His designs were celebrated as the most modern way to gain pleasant, at-tractive environments for city living. Ja-pan, no less enthusiastically than western countries, accepted his ideas and began to turn densely built poorly constructed wooden housing in certain residential areas into medium- or high-rise rein-forced concrete apartment complexes. Japanese architects, too, began to empha-size generous spacing of buildings and plentiful open space in urban planning. All over the world, "new towns" and massive high-rise building complexes

sprouted up, inspired by these new prin-ciples. The new residential complexes did, in fact, guarantee sun, space, and green-ery and made advantageous use of land, and in some cases they were truly successful.

But if to exist means to reside, as the existentialists claim, this kind of city ob-viously failed to provide a sense of fulfill-ment and permanence. Consider the space between high-rise buildings, for ex-ample. It functioned, admittedly, to guar-antee a certain amount of sunshine, at least four hours in the short days of win-ter but was otherwise a kind of void space belonging to no one—it was nega-tive space. As Serge Chermayeff wrote in his book *Community and Privacy,*

. . . Though the logic of this device seemed admirable at first, the enjoyment of such scattered green spaces has turned out to be largely illusory. They are not large enough to act as public parks and not small enough to possess the intimate pleasure of the private garden. Everything belongs to everybody, with the result that nothing actually belongs to, or is enjoyed by, anybody. Their ownership, adminis-tration, and maintenance are neither spe-cifically public nor private. They are leftover voids between gigantic boxes, where sparsely sprinkled adults and chil-dren are equally ill at ease.[8]

People began to ask if it were not possi-ble to divide up such negative space among residents and allot each family a place, no matter how small, to grow flow-ers or vegetables, or set up a workshop so that they might cultivate the "void" in a more constructive, imaginative manner.

In Japan in particular, it is not uncom-mon for a weary commuter to arrive by train at the station nearest his home and set off into a landscape filled with identi-cal, concrete high-rise apartments. If his building is situated some distance away, out of sight, at least the walk through ad-jacent parks may provide some relaxation

94
Exterior view of author's
private sauna
(Photograph: Yutaka
Suzuki)

95
Interior view of author's
private sauna
(Photograph: Yukio
Futagawa)

and pleasure. As it is, the artificiality, sterility, and isolation of the architecture in this environment makes it irrevocably tedious and dull, for the sense of union that characterizes closely built residential communities of one- and two-story houses is absent.

The space between high-rise buildings is neither truly natural nor completely artificial; it is of an awkward size, empty, and vacuous. This may be one reason for the sense of transience and detachment felt by residents of such housing areas. The landscaping of a Japanese public apartment complex, for example, is intended only to be looked at, not to be puttered in. Residents are not allowed to intervene in any way with what little green space they are allowed, and this in itself creates tremendous frustration. Though they live in a "suburban" residential area more than an hour away from the city, they must be content with "natural" surroundings that they can do no more than look at. It is as unmerciful as it is uninspiring.

If high- and medium-rise apartment complexes are built in the heart of the city, they are actually quite desirable and convenient for people who are young, busy, and mobile. But those who wish to settle down permanently feel an impulse to have a "house with a garden." A garden is not a fabricated, artificial place existing only to be looked at; it is a place where a person can come into physical contact with nature, dig in the earth, cultivate plants, put in a tree, sit and eat breakfast, sunbathe, do exercises, read, build a bonfire, or work—an outdoor space of one's very own. If we were to set aside an outside space, even though it may be small, for city people, a space that they can call their own, it may help

to provide them with a deep sense of attachment to nature.

The residential communities of the island towns of the Aegean Sea or in the south of Italy along the Mediterranean coast are especially impressive and revealing in this regard. The towns of such islands as Hydra, Patmos, Rodhos, and Santorini are all composed of low dwellings built on hills sloping toward the sea. The townscapes of these islands are singularly well integrated: the white houses crowded along the winding streets against the clear azure sea and bright blue skies are interwoven in intimate complexity as if of one organic being. And between these houses, in the most unexpected places, one finds small, enclosed exterior spaces with chairs and potted plants set here and there. The gardens are walled in at the back by the slope upon which the houses are built and face on the sea, providing small, yet private outdoor spaces for each home. Sitting in a secluded spot such as this, with some quiet music playing and a glass of wine, perhaps gazing far out upon the Aegean, one can re-live the sense of attachment of these Greek people to the small spaces they have defended throughout the centuries in the face of countless invasions.

The layouts of these towns do not conform with the rules of some architectural standard or urban master plan; they emerged spontaneously by unwritten laws over the centuries.[9] The collective wisdom of a people united by the need for defense produced a solidarity and integrity that is nonexistent in modern planned cities.

Of course, the suggestions these ancient communities offer must be applied to modern design with discretion, for without the most careful and detailed planning, low-housing complexes can easily turn instead into slums. A housing complex should revolve around an "internal order," that is, one generated by internal factors that foster a distinctive townscape and a sense of community attachment, as in case of the Aegean island towns. The scale of a housing complex must be limited; too many units in a complex can impede access by automobile. The towns of the Greek islands I described, with all their variety and rhythm and humanity, could not possibly be transplanted to our modern cities, for automobiles would jam their intimate, winding streets; even if the streets were wider, the best qualities of such a townscape would be lost. Obviously, the internal order of the Italian and Greek towns cannot be adopted unaltered as a model for building on a modern urban scale. The best alternative seems to be small housing complexes of not more than 50 or 60 units, with space set aside among them for landscaping and traffic routes.

Another demand the city is expected to provide is choice in types of dwelling commensurate with family composition, location of schools and work, and other considerations. These needs cannot be answered by massive complexes of medium- or high-rise reinforced concrete apartment buildings, or by unbroken expanses of courtyard houses with postage-stamp gardens. People want a choice of lifestyles, and they seek a niche—a small space—of their own where they can think and act in privacy. These small, private spaces offer replenishing energy needed to manage busy lives, places from which people can set out with confidence for their work places. A balance between "community" and "privacy" is surely the most important concern of the city dweller.

What I have tried to describe here is the small spaces that afford a person the chance for reflection, a habit that is intimately connected with the formation of human character. Some may not be able to imagine themselves as being a fraction of their real size, but they may find it easy to fancy themselves among the fleeting sparrows that disappear into the distant sky. In the world of the imagination, becoming small and going far away are much the same thing. It is perhaps not mistaken to say that, when a man wants to be alone, when he feels the itch to travel, when he longs to see unknown lands, it is "small spaces" for which he is really yearning.

When an architect sits down to design a building, he thinks of space in sketches on a scale of 100 to 1 or 200 to 1. Imagining himself 1/100th or 1/200th of his real size, he moves about in his imaginary architectural space. As if only one centimeter tall, the architect devises spaces in his imagination and divides it into creative existence, bringing the various parts into a unified whole. Nature is originally vague, undefined space. For the purpose of living, it is the architect's task to delimit that vague space into smaller spaces, making the best possible use of the roof, wall, and other architectural elements.

Memorable Spaces

The concept of "imageability" was first defined by Kevin Lynch in 1960 in his book *The Image of the City*.[10] It represents an attempt to perceive the city or townscape, not in terms of concrete features such as buildings, but as images of the structure of those perceived forms. Imageability is not the impression of one single individual, but the image of a city or townscape shared by many people.

The concept grew out of an earlier study conducted by Lynch and Alvin K. Luka-shok reported in a paper, "Some Child-hood Memories of the City."[11] This study sought to identify those elements of the physical environment of a city that make the most lasting impression on children's minds. The results of the questionnaire survey showed that ground surface, wall materials, and trees were among the most memorable elements of urban environ-ments. In another survey recorded in "A Walk around the Block," Lynch and Malcolm Rivkin surveyed the impressions expressed by adult subjects asked to walk around a single block formed by Boylston and Newbury Streets in Boston.[12] Both these studies were based on the assump-tion that the city impresses people with an identifiable image. Lynch writes that the image of a city depends on its "im-ageability," that is, its comprehensibility or "legibility," and its "visibility." This image depends on five major elements: paths, edges, districts, nodes, and land-marks, and the more the imageability of a city is enhanced, the better the environ-ment it becomes.

Kevin Lynch's survey of childhood memories of the city has great signifi-cance, I believe, in discovering the influ-ence of architecture or of townscapes on the formative period of a child's develop-ment. In *La Terre et les reveries du repos*, Gaston Bachelard also discusses the im-portance of the house where a person is born and comments that birthplaces are long remembered, that simply recalling them evokes a sense of comfort and security.[13]

Japanese literary critic Takeo Okuno of-fers some insights on "imageability" in a book on what he calls "primal settings" and their influence on literature. Primal

settings refer to the geographic and social landscapes where writers spend their most impressionable and formative years:

"Primal settings," which are the womb of literature, take shape during an author's early childhood or adolescence. They emerge unconsciously by the seventh or eighth year, from the neighborhood, par-ents, the inside of the home, play places, family members, and friends. These pri-mal settings become deeply implanted in the subconscious and are remembered with increasing nostalgia as a person grows older. Settings not fully understood to a young person, moreover, gradually grow clear in the process of remember-ing. These primal settings are the birth-place of the spirit, the equivalent of the mythological period in the history of mankind.[14]

Okuno studies major Japanese novelists who were brought up in the countryside rather than in large cities like Tokyo and Osaka and who spent their formative years in rural settings rich in local flavor and natural beauty. The landscape for such authors is not simply the local or natural scenery noticed by a passing trav-eler; it contains primal settings to which they are intensely attached, places that are literally part of their flesh-and-blood and which provide constantly recurring themes in their writing. A writer born and reared in the city, says Okuno, can-not match the strength of a country-reared author's bond to his birthplace. He describes, for example, how Yukio Mishima, who passed his most formative period without knowing the beauty of na-ture and the rural landscape, contrived his own fictitious "primal settings" from his reading of Japanese classics and west-ern literature. Okuno recounts the anec-dote that, once out walking with Donald Keene, Mishima pointed to a pine tree and asked the name of the tree. But Mishima is not the only Japanese who has grown up without knowing the indigenous natural landscape. Indeed, from now on there will be many more young people turned out of an urban mold and reared in the man-made landscape of public housing complexes and high-rise apartment buildings. They will all be equally ignorant of the natural world.

In Tokyo before the war, Okuno says, there were landscapes that fostered primal settings, as anyone can attest who has read the works of modern Japanese novelists like Nagai Kafū, Jun'ichirō Tanizaki, or Natsume Sōseki, for in them nostalgic old place names in Tokyo crop up at every turn of the page. Okuno himself was reared in the Ebisu area on the residential heights in central Tokyo that are known as the Yamanote. He recalls that his home faced on a street no more than two meters wide and that a luxuriant growth of twenty or thirty zelkova trees two or three centuries old towered nearby, a wood inhabited by birds, cicadas, and frogs. So at least before the war, even big cities like Tokyo had wooded areas and a sense of continuity with nature that could compete with any in the countryside.

Even in the changing neighborhoods of the Yamanote area, children enjoyed a world apart, a world totally different from school, in vacant lots, sites of former estates, rice paddies, or vegetable fields that have been sold, or areas that had simply never been used for housing or farming. These places were a children's world, where grades in school and the status of parents counted for naught. They were places where children grew up under the eye of urchin bosses who won their position by strength and skill at top spinning and menko. We children of the middle class entered this world timidly, and our presence was tolerated, albeit on the bottommost rungs of that juvenile society. These vacant lots were the real home of Yamanote children; they became their "primal settings."[15]

The neighborhood in which I grew up greatly resembled that which Okuno describes, and many of the things he says strike a nostalgic chord. I was born and reared in Yotsuya in the neighborhood then known as Minami Iga-machi (now Wakaba-chō) near a temple called Sainenji. Then, as now, the area was in the heart of the city, but in those days the temple compound was lorded over by a towering ginko tree and a large myrtle tree that we slipped off every time we climbed. Just next to Minami Iga-machi was Tera-machi, and, as the name suggested, there were many temples along the slope. The Sainenji temple compound was the "lot" for us neighborhood children. There we played, and not only with tops and menko; we did bicycle tricks, climbed trees, engaged in mock battles, played at hide-and-seek and baseball, and staged contests of daring. The cemetery at the side of the compound was always somehow eerie and weird, an eeriness that doubled as dusk fell. There, playing in the "vacant lot" enfolded by the temple compound in the hours between school and nightfall, my primal settings took shape. The fantasies we imagined and contrived in such "lots" were part and parcel of the spiritual birthplace of all Yamanote children.

Intriguingly enough, it is trees, both in my memory and in that of Okuno—large zelkova or ginko trees—that are the inextricable elements of the environment of our childhood. The study of the city by Kevin Lynch bears out the vital importance of trees in the formative period of American children with statistical evidence. We might deduce from this that trees, obviously a crucial element in the development of young people, are far too scarce in the residential areas of cities.

Large trees that have endured wind and snow over decades, even centuries, have accumulated a visible dignity and grace, and their survival over that long period, unbudging from a single spot, bespeaks composure, endurance, and independence. Predestined to a stationary existence, a tree even seems to communicate a sense of receptivity and objectivity and gazes down on children's carefree play with silent severity. Trees like this leave lasting impressions and teach many lessons. For a child, they are much more than "sights" glimpsed along the road; he lives with and knows them in wind and rain and sunshine, from season to season, throughout the years he is growing up.

Kevin Lynch's study also revealed that features such as wall materials and pavements leave strong impressions. My own experience bears this out, for the wall around Sainenji temple and the surface of the sloped street nearby are still vivid memories, although pavements, which may have been important elements of a city landscape in other countries, were not so very common in Japan in those days. For Italian children, on the other hand, who grow up playing in streets and church squares, primal settings must often be associated with the hard surfaces of stone steps and pavements.

Recently, in a survey of childhood memories of forty students in the Architecture Department at the University of Tokyo, no less than 25 percent mentioned trees or tree climbing: three oak trees, a Himalaya cedar, a camphor tree, a chestnut, a ginko—and in every case they were immense and dignified. Those brought up in rural areas often mentioned streams and riverbanks, while urban children referred to sloping streets, stone stairways, and vacant lots. These

young people apparently still have "primal settings" closely associated with the natural environment, but we are entering an age when children will spend their formative years increasingly in reinforced concrete apartment buildings in the company of nothing more natural and alive than a television set, and it makes one stop to think: What kind of people will be produced by such an artificial environment? Will these young people be a new kind of human being that accumulates all knowledge through the experiences of others provided by the media, especially by television?

Now, putting aside "primal settings," let me turn to the subject of the Japanese townscape. The Japanese city is a notoriously difficult subject to portray in writing. Just as in the case of Japanese artists who, though they may paint numerous canvases of the city while studying in Europe, seem somehow unable to capture the townscapes of their own country, the reason may be that the primary profile of the townscape formed by the walls of buildings is so obscured and overriden by the secondary profile in Japanese cities, with its plethora of protruding fixtures and miscellany, that it cannot be coherently described. Takeo Okuno writes that the solid masonry architecture of Europe and America is relatively easy to portray, while Japanese cities do not lend themselves to distinctive literary images. No matter how detailed the description, it does not communicate a meaningful picture. We can speculate that this is because western townscapes are not dominated by the unfixed, temporary elements of a secondary profile and their masonry architecture presents a clearly defined profile.

In prewar works of literature by major Japanese writers like Natsume Sōseki, place names in the Hongo area of Tokyo, for example, crop up frequently, and the atmosphere of that part of the city is lovingly and faithfully portrayed. In contemporary fiction, according to Okuno, the city does not present such a distinctive, fixed image.

Japanese fiction is not lacking in portrayals of cities or townscapes because authors are unskilled or inept. One has only to examine the recent rash of novels by Japanese set in foreign countries to see that they can and do draw the cities of other countries with an impressive flair for detail and imagery. The names of streets and boulevards are recorded almost to the point of fetishism, and the details of churches and squares, parks and residential areas are set down faithfully. Not only that, they evoke with impressive accuracy the atmosphere—or rather the milieu—of daily life in those cities.[16]

In order for a space perceived to have meaning for the perceiver, there must be some established, shared model that serves as a reference. But the Japanese townscape has no system, no fixed schemes or patterns. Its configuration is dominated by the secondary profile, and an explicit "figure" does not emerge, so a structural perception of space is not possible. The perception of space as it actually is and the formation of an image of a townscape in the context of a fixed social and cultural setting are two different processes. Because a townscape is a concrete entity, it is always subject to direct perception, but whether it registers as a recognizable, fixed imagistic structure is another matter. Occupied by much that is temporary and lightly constructed, there is little in the helter-skelter arrangement of buildings in a Japanese townscape that contributes to a systematic image.

When it comes to comprehensibility, not only of portions of the city such as single streets but the framework as a whole—its imageability—some cities are very difficult to grasp, while others leave a clear and indelible impression. Some have no particular rationale, they simply sprawl across the countryside. Certain districts may be easily grasped; others are confusing no matter how many times one visits.

Paris is a city known to all. It makes skillful use of the Seine River, which admirably performs the role of "edge" in the sense referred to in Lynch's analysis, dividing the city into Right Bank and Left Bank. The Notre-Dame cathedral commands the Seine from the Ilê de la Cité, connected to the rest of the city by a series of bridges. Without the Seine, these landmarks would be less memorable by far. The Eiffel Tower, Notre-Dame, the Opera house, the Madeleine cathedral, the Pantheon, all are famous features that contribute to the imageability of Paris. Even the chestnut and other trees that line the streets are elements that help to create the unforgettable impression of this city.

Tokyo has its Sumida River spanned by many bridges, its Honganji temple in Tsukiji, the National Theatre, Imperial Palace, the Tokyo Tower, and Meiji Shrine. At close look, its streets are planted with ginko, platanus, zelkova, and maple trees. Yet none of these features seems to be developed sufficiently to give the city real imageability.

If Paris had been rebuilt according to Le Corbusier's Plan Voisin, like the planned capitals of Brasilia, or Chandigarh, how would it seem? With a clearly defined scheme filled with open space like that of Brasilia, Paris could hardly have become the world city it is today. During the period of economic expansion in the 1960s, serious thought was given to innovations in the world's cities, and designers came up with schemes for cities in the air, floating cities, and tower cities. At the same time the movement to preserve outstanding architectural masterpieces and historical townscapes gained momentum, and efforts to preserve and develop established cities took on new urgency. Architects slowly began to replace their visions of building new cities or carrying out massive reconstruction of old ones with more realistic alternatives.

The image of the city advocated by Le Corbusier and others of the Modern Architecture Movement turned away from the continuity of traditional cities and townscapes; cities were envisioned as consisting of high-rise building complexes placed in spacious expanses and connected by super expressways. Projects were begun in urban development and new city core designs such as Paris's Defense Project and the complex of high-rise buildings in Tokyo's Shinjuku area. Architects originally dreamed of creating places of *"soleil, l'éspace, verdue,"* as well as speed and functionalism. But, as these projects neared completion, doubts began to emerge about just who the inhuman, sterile urban contrivances that had been built were intended for in the first place. With seeming disregard for the pedestrian, they involve distances much too long to walk comfortably. Designed mainly with the automobile in mind, they are in many cases negotiable only by the young and modern. There is no place for the elderly or the handicapped, and no measures taken to ensure humanity and peace of mind. Here the streets are kinder to automobiles than to pedestrians. There are places in these "planned cities" where the pedestrian's path to nearby, readily visible places is blocked or extremely roundabout. In the rebuilt portion of Shinjuku,

for example, a huge multilevel intersection blocks the way to nearby buildings, and pedestrians must go completely around it. Such problems as this have caused much skepticism about the Modern Architecture Movement. The composition of exterior space must be carefully planned to divide up the immense spaces of cities into small spaces designed on a human scale. The design of spaces between buildings should be planned to facilitate figure reversal in the Gestalt sense and develop a townscape truly designed for people. A city deserves to be a place that is memorable.

5

*Townscapes of
the World*

Townhouses of Paddington and Kyoto

Paddington is an old residential district in the city of Sydney composed of Victorian-style terrace houses. Once a virtual slum, in recent years this area has become the focus of new efforts at repair and restoration and has rapidly grown into a distinctive community of special appeal to artists and intellectuals (figure 96).

The Paddington terrace houses are mostly two-story, common-wall row houses, sandwiched together on long, slender sites. Their second-story balconies are fitted with cast-iron handrails of decorative Victorian-style openwork. Occupying a 400 acre complex whose history goes back to 1804, they were first built in a plain Georgian style, and soon thereafter adapted to a more ornate Victorian taste that still prevails. One attraction of these terrace houses is that, while they are built on very small lots with no wasted space, the interiors are still fairly spacious. Their small inner gardens introduce a sense of seasonal change, and the ornamental openwork handrails provide continuity, yet with a certain variety, that serves to bring the townscape into a unified whole (figure 97).

The streets of this district average more than 10 meters wide, and the D/H ratio between the height of the buildings and the breadth of the streets is a generous 1.5, giving the community a feeling of sunny, quiet comfort, while the houses built as they are make for a highly integrated townscape. Because the building space is so efficiently used, the streets are comparatively wide, even where the population density is quite high.

Upon entering the gates of these terrace houses from the street, one finds a tiny front garden to the side of the steps to the front door. The width of one row house ranges from a lean 3.5 meters to

96
Townscape of
Paddington, Sydney,
Australia
(Photograph: Yoshinobu
Ashihara)

97
Inner garden of
Paddington terrace
houses
(Photograph: Yoshinobu
Ashihara)

several times that width, but the depth or length is fixed by the nature of the site. The living room windows are typically situated to the side of the front door. Inside, the front living room adjoins a dining area facing the small inner garden at the side of the house. In most, a folding door between the two main rooms allows for plenty of light and ventilation of the living and dining areas. Usually, right ahead of the front door is a flight of stairs to the second floor. The upstairs is divided into several bedrooms, with the master bedroom opening out onto the balcony overlooking the street. From inside, all the different ironwork handrails on these balconies are not particularly noticeable, but from the street they each present a distinctive and attractive motif for the townscape (figure 98). Expensive, carefully wrought works of art, their lacework patterns give the houses a pleasing quality of transparency.

Since there is no leftover space between the houses, the facades form a continuous line, and the streets emerge as Gestalt figures creating an impressive townscape like the Italian townscapes described earlier. Australia is a spacious country, and elsewhere in Sydney residential sites are of a more generous size, often with large front yards. The Paddington terrace houses reflect the Victorian ethos of solid middle-class working people who recreated on Sydney's slopes a community in the image of their homes back in England. Only since World War II have architects and connoisseurs of the arts sought to bring back to life this modest type of dwelling, whose cozy proportions demonstrate the importance of a "castle all one's own" even in an expansive country like Australia.

Japan's counterpart to the Paddington terrace house is its *machiya*, or town-

98
Cast-iron handrail in Victorian style, Paddington (Photograph: Yoshinobu Ashihara)

houses, best seen in the ancient capital Kyoto. There, however, the streets are only 6.5 meters wide, producing a D/H factor of around 1, which makes the whole much lower and closer together on what might be called a human scale. Corresponding to Paddington's cast-iron handrails, the windows on the first story of these Kyoto townhouses are uniformly fitted with wooden lattices. The curving, Victorian lines and flowery iron lace that give Paddington its distinctive flavor are replaced in Kyoto by the simple, straight lines of these wooden lattices, a common architectural element that serves as a strong unifying link in the townscape (figure 99). Because of the constrictions of narrow lots, the house plans are relatively uniform, with the main entrances and front sitting rooms facing on the street. The rooms, which are divided by *fusuma* panels, are laid out in a straight line from front to back, continuing all the way to the back garden. Between the buildings are small passageways leading to the back gardens and stairways to the second floors (figure 100). An authoritative study of Kyoto's townhouses shows that their average area is 133.5 square meters, with the house occupying 64.6 percent of the lot and having a total floor space of 131.6 square meters. Yet the population density of these dwellings is comparatively higher than the 300 people-per-hectare capacity of medium-rise public housing complexes in Japan. Moreover, the total floor of one townhouse is 2.5 times larger than a unit in a public housing complex (52 square meters), and this even includes the small private garden.[1]

The terrace houses of Paddington and the *machiya* of Kyoto demonstrate that an elongated architectural style can be quite conducive to an appealing townscape. These are attractive dwellings, particularly suited to cities where there is a premium on land space and energy resources. They incorporate a measure of private outdoor space, even though quite limited in size, as well as relatively comfortable indoor space through an efficient use of the site, and these places are much healthier to live in than public housing complexes. The modest gardens concealed behind Kyoto's *machiya* have a beauty and tranquility totally unknown to passersby, and, though diminutive, are of sufficient size to be enjoyed by the residents. These gardens share the qualities of "small spaces" I mentioned in chapter 4. Although they are not meant to be entered, they offer a bit of nature which is relaxing to look at and which communicates a sense of the seasons (figure 101). Certainly the townhouse is a type of residential architecture that deserves much further study.

The Integrated Cities of Apulia, the Aegean Isles, and Isfahan

In the Apulia region southeast of Rome at the heel of Italy lies the town of Alberobello, famous for its conical roofed houses built entirely of stone. Part of the town, an area of about 37 acres, has been set aside by the government as a national monument (figures 102 and 103). The stone dwellings to be found here, with their conical roofs of stone, are called *trulli*, and they are quite fairylike in appearance. They are whitewashed up to the eaves, and the peaks of the roofs built of flat stones are whitewashed and topped by decorative stone pinnacles.

The interiors of these *trulli*, though small, are quite comfortable, with thick stone walls shutting off the outside and creating a solid sense of security. Like the exteriors, the interior walls are immaculately whitewashed, although in some the

99
Townhouse of Kyoto
(Photograph: Yoshinobu
Ashihara)

100
Plan of typical Kyoto
townhouse
(From Noboru
Shimamura, *Kyō no machiya*)

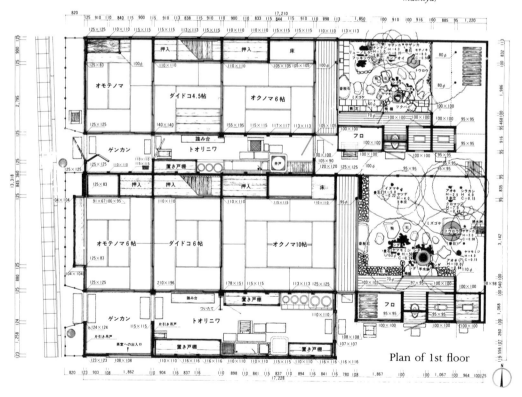

Plan of 1st floor

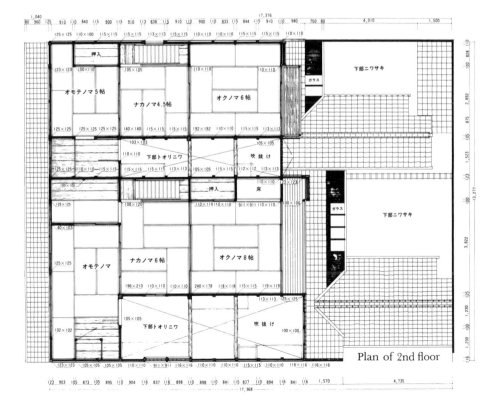

Plan of 2nd floor

押入

オモテノマ5帖　ナカノマ4.5帖　オクノマ6帖　下部ニワサキ

ガラス

下部トオリニワ　吹抜け

押入　床

ガラス

下部ニワサキ

オモテノマ　ナカノマ6帖　オクノマ8帖

下部トオリニワ　吹抜け

101
Small inner garden
(*tsuboniwa*) of Kyoto
townhouse
(Photograph: Haruzō
Ōhashi)

stones of the vaulted ceilings are left exposed. Openings to the outside are limited to the front door and several small windows. Although such stone architecture would hardly be feasible in the high humidity of Japan, the *trulli* are cool and cozy, with the same inexplicable fascination that is experienced in a cave.

Not far from Alberobello, passing through Locorotondo, Martina Franca, and other small communities, there is the small country town of Cisternino, in medieval times a castle town whose character is a source of immense fascination to a devotee of the aesthetics of the townscape. Cisternino is the epitome of an integrated city that possesses an internal order of its own; it embodies the concept of a city as one immense architectural unit which has long been part of my thinking.

Other medieval walled cities I have seen in Tuscany, such as San Gimignano and Assisi, have impressed me with their internal order. But despite the unified, closely built and contiguous architecture in those cities, the individual character of each building quite obviously derives from the period in which it was built. Like the townhouses of Kyoto, they were built with methods and materials of a standard type, yet asserting their separate heritages. What is remarkable about Cisternino is that, because the outer walls of all the houses are carefully whitewashed, they give the appearance of uniform vintage, a major factor in the total impression of solid integrity. The town is an immense maze of whitewashed buildings and paved streets unified in a single, intricate monolith of stone, and riddled with tunneling streets and external stairways. To come upon a town such as this, looking like something out of my own fantasy, was an unforgettable thrill.

The older quarter of Cisternino is encircled by the castle wall, and the houses inside were added on and filled into the space in such density that quite often exterior staircases were built to reach the residences constructed on top of existing ones (figures 104 and 105). Atop arches built over the streets are poised yet more houses, and the front stoops and verandas of houses turn up in the most surprising places. Unlike a planned town, the houses were built over a period of time wherever there was space, in every unused corner, between, and even atop the earliest buildings. Confined by the encircling castle walls, the city could not spread outward, and every available bit of space is used to the utmost advantage.

In the center of this old city is the Piazza Vittorio Emanuelle, a small square where, in the time-honored Italian custom of the *corso*, the people of the town congregate for conversation and relaxation. Facing on the square, there was a barbershop run by a man named Nicola Greco whom Jane Jacobs would have called a "street watcher," for he kept a close eye on all the events that went on in the town. The arrival of a camera-dangling Japanese constituted a major event in that remote place, where even Italian visitors from the Rome area are rare, and my presence was known throughout the town in a matter of minutes.[2]

The uniform whitewashing of the building exteriors that gives towns like Cisternino their outstanding sense of aesthetic unity is found not only in southern Italy, but in Spain, Greece, and North Africa. For sense of unity and immaculateness, perhaps none can surpass those on the isles in the Aegean Sea. Against the deep blue of sea and sky and the dry landscape of Mediterranean coasts, the whitewashed dwellings climbing their slopes

102
Townscape of
Alberobello, Italy
(Photograph: Yoshinobu
Ashihara)

103
Street map of
Alberobello, Italy
(From Edward Allen,
Stone Shelters)

104
Exterior staircases in
Cisternino
(Photograph: Yoshinobu
Ashihara)

105
Street map of Cisternino
(From Edward Allen,
Stone Shelters)

present a striking contrast. In defense against the glaring Mediterranean sunshine, windows are extremely small and few in number. Modern architecture, with its expanses of glass and steel, would seem alien in this region and would ill-adapt to the hot, sunny climate.

The island of Hydra lies 60 kilometers to the south of Athens, just off the Peloponnesian peninsula. The techniques of building towns on slopes facing the sea, which became quite sophisticated in these Greek islands, developed as a defense against the recurrent attacks of marauding pirates that punctuate the history of the region. Today, however, the tightly knit townscapes have become a tourist attraction, and appreciation of low-built housing clusters like those in these Aegean towns has spread.

The measures devised for defense in Hydra are impressive. Streets are of two types: horizontal cross-streets following the contours of the hills, and vertical streets climbing radially from the square on the edge of the quay where all town activities focus and originate. Most of the vertical streets are stepped, surely in partial effort to slow the assault of invaders unfamiliar with the terrain. The streets following the contour lines are filled with sudden turns and blind curves, although most are without steps. In Japan the counterpart to this strategically devised street system may be found in its medieval castle-towns with their maze of streets winding through the protective ring of retainers's houses around the fortified castle. The street pattern in Hydra makes it easy to move from the residential areas to the central square below, one simply descends the stepped streets, all of which lead unerringly to the central quay. But it is much more difficult to find one's way in the opposite direction, for the stone retaining walls of the longitudinal streets were planned as double- and triple-layered defenses against invaders. The streets are no wider than necessary, usually just enough for two beasts of burden loaded with goods to pass; the main intersections of the longitudinal and vertical streets are marked by shade-giving trees.

Quite apart from the scenic beauty of this Mediterranean region, its towns demonstrate much we can learn from in improving our modern living styles. One is keenly aware of a warmth and ingenuity in architectural design, often contrived originally in the interests of defense, that tends to be overlooked in the planning of modern cities. The town of Hydra is finely integrated, as if it were a single, cohesive dwelling with the square at the quay as its living room and the streets as its corridors. It is an intimate, comfortable town of familial solidarity that gives it an internal order. The distinctive residential building style, which has been carefully studied by Constantine E. Michaelides, follows a standard spatial sequence, from an entrance set back from the public area of the street, progressing to an inner private exterior space and then to interior space.[3] As in Italian towns the houses are built directly on the streets, but, upon entering the front door a visitor finds himself inside a small garden like a roofless entry hall that leads to an inner door to the house itself. Although at first this townscape seems typical of Italy, the private inner gardens are characteristic of Spanish residential style. Land is used intensively, and, while plots are small, there is no wasted space around the buildings and homes have many rooms of spacious dimensions.

Perhaps what is most charming about the townscapes of these Greek island communities is the sloping configuration of houses built on the steep incline of the hills. The roofs of lower buildings become the terraces of those above, and these roof terraces provide exquisite panoramas of sky and sea. From the ocean, looking up at such towns, the pure white houses seem to float in overlapping profusion, sharply contrasting with the somber colors of the local terrain. One is conscious of the whitewashing in these towns, which seems to assert human will against the barren dryness of the land.

A spectacular example of this kind of townscape is to be found on the island of Santorini (figure 106), an island located about halfway between Athens and Crete. Its main town, Thira, is almost too beautiful to be of this world. Knowing how gloomy Hydra is in winter, I timed my two visits to coincide with summer, when the islands are bathed in a strong sunlight that sets off the beauty of the landscape. Thira is built near the peak of the west slope on a 300-meter precipice. In the early morning, as ships begin to arrive and anchor in the inlet directly below, the town is silhouetted against the rising sun, a sight that never fails to be impressive. Cargo is transferred from the ships onto barges that carry them to the wharf where a crowd of donkeys awaits. Like Venice, this town has no automobiles, and on the steep slopes stone stairs wind in zigzag patterns. The donkeys negotiate them with ease, carrying people and goods up to the town.

The distinctive quality of Thira is above all the integrated composition of its clusters of low, solidly white houses constructed in overlapping profusion along its steep sloping streets. The houses in this region of the dry zone are partially dug into the side of the cliff, making them pleasantly cool within. Since rainfall is so scarce, the roofs are all flat and serve as the terraces of the houses above. These terraces are perfect examples of "small spaces," facing west toward the open sea, their backs guarded by sheer walls, making them places of inexpressible calm and serenity. The unobstructed panoramas from these terraces are among the world's most superb.

Now, leaving the blue Aegean behind, let us cross the Arabian deserts to Iran, where both nature and the character of dwellings are totally different.

Isfahan is located about 300 kilometers south of Teheran, approximately midway between the present capital and Persepolis. Built by Darius I as the capital city of the Achaemenid empire, it is among the most exotic of Persia's ancient cities. It is for the most part a dry, desert zone, and diverse life-styles share a common foundation in the traditions of Islamic culture.

Methods of building in the dry zone are adapted to the climate. Wood, as a structural material strong in tensile and bending moment, is convenient for posts and beams, as well as furniture, doors, roofing, and siding. But in a region where there are almost no trees, it constitutes a luxury that ordinary people can hardly afford. Except for a rainy region on the south side of the Caspian Sea, dwellings are made mostly of sun-dried mud brick (a claylike mud formed into uniform bricks and dried in rows in the sun). Primitive as they may seem, these mud houses effectively block out severe heat, a providential asset in this desert climate. On the other hand, in terms of structural dynamics, sun-dried brick weathers quickly; it is dusty and prone to flake. The buildings, moreover, are dark, almost gloomy, and lack a sense of immaculateness and brightness that attracts us to the

106
Townscape in Thira on
Santorini
(Photograph: Yoshinobu
Ashihara)

whitewashed, masonry dwellings of the Mediterranean Sea region. In contrast to the explicit lines formed by buildings made of wood or stone, and to the aura of solidity that comes from hard materials, houses made of mud brick have rounded, dulled profiles and a sense of fragility resulting from the soft and brittle nature of the materials. The houses of the common people of Iran, unlike the bleached dwellings of the Mediterranean seacoasts that symbolize man's struggle against nature, seem indistinguishable from the landscape. In Isfahan these mud-brick buildings are still common. The sole presence of human-contrived color in these mud houses is the ubiquitous "Persian rug," used everywhere to cover the earthen floors. Lacking wood for materials, tables for eating and beds for sleeping are absent; all daily activities take place on the brightly colored carpets.

When I first visited Isfahan in 1970, I found the layout of the town, the lettering on the signs, the expressions of the people totally strange and different. And yet there was *something* that struck a compelling cord. It was something in the culture of the dry belt that told me that, for one brought up in this severe environment, it was a perfectly logical kind of townscape. Quite apart from whether it suited me, I decided then that I must make a study of this town. Thinking back on Isfahan after I had left, I realized that in all its parts—its brilliantly colored, mosaic-encrusted mosques, mazelike bazaars, and mud-brick houses plastered to the earth—it formed a mysteriously harmonious whole. This townscape represented the most eloquent testimony possible to the way the people of this region comprehend the landscape and climate in which they live; it revealed how it had been built over the centuries from

the fabric of Islamic culture. With a new interest in this organic process, I returned to Isfahan in 1977 and at last began to gain a better grasp of the meaningful aspects of its townscape.

An aerial view of Isfahan shows how the city is formed, with houses packed together along narrow streets (figure 107). It might be more accurate to say that it consists of streets threading through a dense throng of houses. All the houses are built opening inward, onto inner courtyards, so that walls line the streets. Architect Kōji Yagi writes that,

In inland areas where it is dry, and day and night temperatures vary considerably, the inner courtyard style of dwelling is advisable. Ventilation is not particularly necessary, but medium-sized windows are needed to let in sunshine in the winter months; a compact plan for the community is preferable. Heavy material of high thermal capacity used for walls and roof takes advantage of the natural time lag of heat transfer in which the warmth of daytime carries over to counteract the cool winter nights. As a result room temperature at night is higher than the external temperature, although in winter some artificial heat must be added. On the other hand, for the long and severely hot summers, spaces are provided for sleeping out of doors on the roofs, or verandas, or in the inner courtyards.[4]

I also went to see the mud-brick houses of farmers living in the suburbs of Isfahan (figure 108). The farmers greeted me with unexpected warmth and invited me to join them at tea, this particular beverage prepared in a large silver samovar (figure 109). As mentioned earlier, because wood is scarce and costly, tables, shelves, and beds are nonexistent. A front door made of wood is considered a precious possession. The floors are covered with Persian rugs. Shelves, formed by carving niches into the earthen walls, provide storage places for dishes and utensils. Bedding consists of quilts and blankets, rolled up

107
Aerial view of Isfahan
(From Nader Ardalan,
The Sense of Unity)

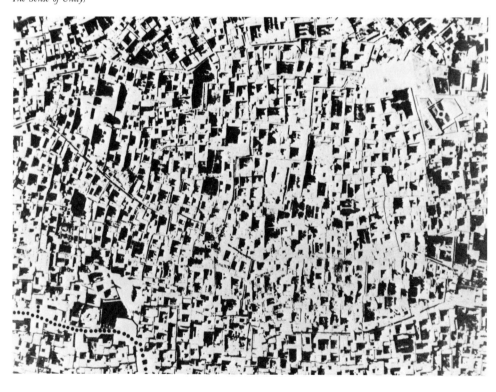

108
Rural dwelling of sun-
dried mud brick in Iran
(Photograph: Yoshinobu
Ashihara)

109
Interior of rural
dwelling in Iran
(Photograph: Yoshinobu
Ashihara)

in one corner of the floor until needed. Entering the dusky, earth-colored spaces of these houses, one can understand why it is that the people in this region weave their rugs in bright colors, and decorate the domes of mosques with kaleidoscopic mosaic. Certainly these are ways of counteracting the harsh, drab natural environment in which they live. The "Persian rug" is not a luxury, nor a collector's item; but a necessity of life of unique spiritual significance.

In Isfahan, where the houses are quite westernized and equipped with electricity, life-styles are somewhat different, but the same fundamental principle of courtyard-style dwellings prevails. They have a kind of "internal order," suggesting one immense architectural unit, not unlike that which characterizes the uniformly white-washed buildings of towns like Cisternino and Santorini. Those white buildings have an integrity of form that is set off clearly against the grayness of the surrounding landscape. The earth-colored houses of Isfahan also cluster in closely integrated units, but, because they are the same color as the earth upon which they stand, it takes somewhat longer to recognize the peculiar internal order that governs them. Given a few days to acclimatize, the amazing integrity and order of this city cannot fail to impress one, no matter what his religion or ethnic background. Save for the dazzling, fanciful mosques, the city seems one immense architectural complex rising literally out of the earth itself. This massive conglomerate of earthen dwellings serenely and firmly determines the townscape of the city; even the towering mosques are ultimately absorbed and integrated into its total context.

In the mid-seventh century the Persian empire ruled by the Sassan dynasty was overthrown by rising Arab power, launching at the end of that century the first blossoming of Islamic architecture. Middle Islamic architecture, which flourished during the Seljuk empire of the eleventh century, is exemplified in Isfahan's Masjid-i-Jami, the "Friday Mosque." In the latter part of the sixteenth century the Shah Abbas moved the capital of his empire to Isfahan and built a new district on the southwestern side of the existing city in a massive project of city planning. In olden days the city was completely surrounded by a wall as in other cities. The center of the city is the Maidan-i-Shah, the "Square of Kings," built by Shah Abbas. The bazaar that links this square with the Friday Mosque, built in the Seljuk period, provides a fascinating glimpse of Isfahan as it was long ago. The linear configuration of the bazaar, the very backbone of the city, has been meticulously diagramed by architect Nader Ardalan to show the governing relationships of this townscape.[5] Let us follow his map along the 1.6 kilometer path that leads from the Friday Mosque to the Square of Kings (figures 110 and 111, parts a through l).

The Masjid-i-Jami is the most prominent mosque in Isfahan. It contains a rectangular courtyard, approximately 50 by 70 meters, where worshippers gather to pray, kneeling in the direction of Mecca. On the south side is a huge dome flanked by two elegant minarets. The courtyard is surrounded by a two-story arcade, forming a completely enclosed space. The mosaic tile of the mosque, its predominant color deep blue, is dazzlingly beautiful. One might think that, without the focus for architectural space provided by the cross in Christianity or statuary in Buddhism, these religious structures would lack coherence. But this function is

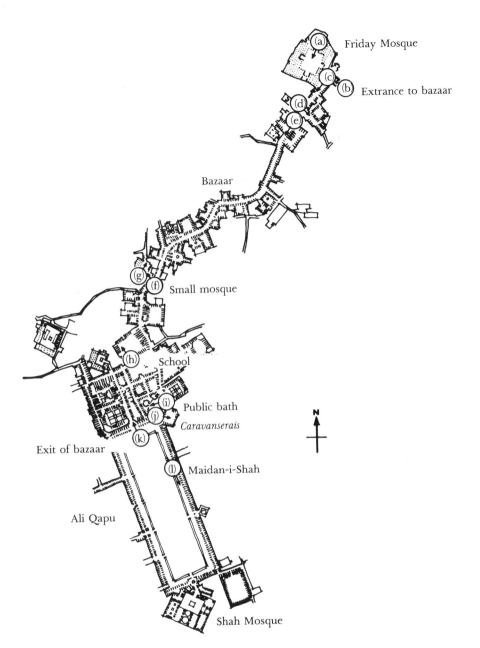

Friday Mosque

Extrance to bazaar

Bazaar

Small mosque

School

Public bath
Caravanserais

Exit of bazaar

Maidan-i-Shah

Ali Qapu

Shah Mosque

110
Map of Isfahan's bazaar
area: the letters show
points from which
photographs in parts (a)
through (l) were taken
(Source: Nader Ardalan,
The Sense of Unity)

(a)
Masjid-i-Jami ("Friday
Mosque")

(b)
Straight ahead is the
Friday Mosque, to the
left the bazaar

(c)
The bazaar

(d)
Inside the bazaar

(e)
Interior of the bazaar

(f)
Entrance to the small
mosque

(g)
Inside the small mosque

(h)
School

(i)
Public bathhouse

(j)
Caravanserais

(k)
Exit of the bazaar

(I)
Maidan-i-Shah ("Square
of Kings")

fulfilled by the orientation toward faraway Mecca; the sun-filled enclosure surrounded by the brilliantly colored arcades is a fitting form for this desert climate and the Islamic religion. At close examination, one finds that this mosque is without doors or separating walls; the space is completely contiguous. Some parts stand in bright sunlight; others lie in shadow. Contrasts are strong—brightness and dark, light and shadow, black and white; there is no mingled, ambiguous color. The space is explicit and distinct. When standing in this mosque, I experienced a refreshing sensation of lightness, as if disembodied.

The roof of the bazaar is vaulted in sun-dried mud brick, and inside, shafts of sunlight reach down through skylights to the shops lining both sides of the passageway like electric spotlights. The shops offer a profusion of daily necessities—clothing, food, cooking utensils, and other wares native to the area. For those accustomed only to manufactured goods, it is a scene that harks back to the markets of ancient Persia. The main trunk of the bazaar branches off among the shops into side streets. Almost all these byways take one into buildings built around inner courts: small mosques, schools, public bathhouses, and *caravanserais* (commercial depots where goods are unloaded from pack animals). These cluster along the length of the bazaar, but compared to its incessant din, seem part of a different world. Still other side streets lead off into residential areas, where the houses are all of courtyard design and nothing can be seen of the activities within.

The bazaar offers an experience of the five senses unlike any to be had in the shopping streets of western countries. A melange of sound, not echoing, for the walls are made of sound-absorbing earth,

but direct, fills the space. The din is intense, and yet it is not high-pitched or piercing, but dulled, as if resounding inside a huge pot. A blend of smells is almost mystical, mingling the fragrances of local spices and incense as well as dust and refuse.

At the end of the bazaar the space abruptly opens out. Suddenly, as if emerging from a dark tunnel into the light, you are in an immense square filled with space and sunlight. This is the northern end of the Square of Kings. It extends 165 meters east and west and 510 meters north and south.[6] The size of this space is far bigger than the 58-by-148-meter average among the largest European squares described by Camillo Sitte.[7] The distance between buildings facing each other compared to their height (D/H) is as much as 10 on the short side, proportions quite obviously not conducive to the sense of enclosure and intimacy one feels in certain Italian piazzas. And yet, upon emerging from the dark bazaar, its spaciousness may be far more desirable. The square is surrounded by a two-story arcade that may be favorably compared with any of the finest Renaissance arcades in Italy. While the D/H factor is very great, the arcade imparts to the square a sense of rhythm and integrity. Today the first floor of the arcade is filled with shops while the second consists of arched niches painted in white plaster. From the rear, they are simple earth-colored mud brick. These concave arches are repeated in intervals of uniform measurement around the square, an accent to its regular shape that contrasts sharply with the disorderly bazaar.

Two mosques open off this square, touching it at 45-degree angles. That on the east end is the Masjid-i-Shaykh Lutfullah, and the other, on the south, is the

Masjid-i-Shah. The eastern mosque is small, without courtyard or minarets; that on the south is the crowning touch to this majestic square. Over its arched gate two minarets beckon to worshippers; as the path turns a sharp 45 degree angle, across the courtyard, where worshippers kneel in prayer facing Mecca, rise the brilliantly colored minarets and the dome. To the west stands the Ali Qapu palace, from whose upper level ceremonies conducted in the square can be viewed. This pavilion is constructed using wooden pillars, giving it a transparency and high profile that contrasts with the solid, heavy qualities of the lower buildings that surround it.

While every year the cities of the world bow to the forces of internationalization and uniformity, Isfahan lives on as a symbol of the distinctive culture of this dry belt region. It is a townscape growing out of and responding to local climate and tradition. Some may need time to understand the rich human qualities of this city, for it is not built of stone, like the familiar buildings of Italy and Greece. But like stone, mud brick is a material indigenous to its area.

Chandigarh and Japan's Shopping Streets

The opposite extremes in townscape configuration can be found, on the one hand, in urban areas where buildings are positioned far apart, following the principle of *"soleil, l'éspace, verdue,"* and, on the other, in streets crowded on both sides by a contiguous row of buildings. A good example of the former is Chandigarh designed by Le Corbusier. As a demonstration of the latter, we shall study the lively sidestreets of Japan's busy city centers.

Le Corbusier wrote voluminously on city planning, but his success in rendering theory into reality on the scale of cities, as he did with pure forms of residential architecture in his early work, must be reconsidered. Chandigarh, the new capital city in India's northern state of Punjab, is one example of a city planned by Le Corbusier that became a reality. The original, basic plan was made by Albert Mayer, who was deeply influenced by the garden-city concept advocated by Ebenezer Howard and others in the 1920s and 1930s. Mayer's plan was based on a series of neighborhood units 900 by 450 meters in size, each of which was to be furnished with elementary schools, shopping areas, and small parks. He also worked out a traffic plan with separate systems for pedestrians and automobile traffic. It was to be a beautiful city endowed with generous quantities of open space. But the concept of the garden city had developed in the West, and grave doubts arose about its appropriateness to the social, economic, and cultural conditions of India.

Le Corbusier was commissioned to succeed Mayer in realizing the plans for the new city. In 1951, visiting the Punjab for the first time, he made several major changes in Mayer's basic plan. He expanded the size of the neighborhood blocks to 1,200 by 800 meters and changed the curved street pattern to a grid of straight streets, introducing what he called the 7V traffic system. This traffic hierarchy, dividing the streets and thoroughfares into seven categories, seemed in theory ideal, but it is difficult to evaluate because the vast majority of local people do not even own automobiles. Today, with the oil crisis, it is hard to tell when, if ever, families will be able to own private cars in India in sufficient numbers to demonstrate the expected potential of the

7V system. Thus, despite the city's sophisticated traffic system, most people are forced to walk across staggeringly long distances in order to attend to the most routine business.

In general India is a nation where automobiles and public transportation facilities are limited, and people go about their business largely on foot or by bicycle. In Chandigarh the main office buildings are spaced very far apart, and the expanses that must be covered between buildings have proved a source of severe inconvenience, especially in the summer when intense heat makes the unshaded walkways almost unendurable. The careful separation of pedestrian and motorized traffic, high-speed throughways, and flyover ramps are, at least for the immediate future, superfluous. As a design model it measures up to any of the so-called "new towns" of the West, but it cannot be denied that this is a distinctively Indian garden city. In a society where many people walk barefoot and transportation is conducted by manpower-driven pedicabs and rickshaws, I am convinced that the garden city concept is sadly misplaced. Chandigarh's residents, forced to live in the midst of a westernized urban setting that is completely oblivious to the local climate and to economic and social conditions, can only grit their teeth and endure their hardships.

Let us take a look at Chandigarh's capital complex, the northernmost sector of the city that encompasses the secretariat, assembly building, high court, and governor's official residence, with an open area scattered with a number of monuments. Le Corbusier put the greatest effort into this part of the design. He positioned the buildings by manipulating purely geometric shapes. He started out by dividing two 800-meter squares set side by side into 400-meter squares, within which he located major buildings. Then he shifted two of the smaller squares 100 meters to the west, to be set aside for various monuments, in an effort to provide a focus for the plan. Le Corbusier was above all an artist, and in the spacing of the buildings, visual perspective was the decisive consideration. He prepared 8-meter poles painted with white and black stripes and affixed with a white flag. After first formulating a preliminary sketch, he visited the site in person and had the poles positioned where the corners of the buildings were to be. When he found that the buildings would be too far apart, he went on to adjust, not through scientific calculations but on the basis of *feel*, until he finally achieved the proportions and relationships between the buildings that he wanted. With traditions like that of the medieval European cities, with their richly human and spontaneous ingenuity, and going back to the elegant symmetry of the Renaissance and Baroque periods, not to mention the scientific and technological achievements of modern architecture, it seems curious that an individual architect should choose to spend hours in the blazing tropical sun of India's flatlands with crude 8-meter poles trying to intuitively confirm a geometrically manipulated plan.

Examined firsthand, the buildings stand far apart, seeming in total isolation. The distance between the secretariat at one end and the high court at the other, for example, is about 700 meters, an expanse that cannot possibly become positive architectural space. Even though the buildings in a townscape may form the "figure," and the areas in between the "ground," there is no possibility of figure-ground reversal if the figures are too monumental. In other words, in Le Corbusier's architectural space the Gestalt phenomenon does not apply to the spaces between the buildings. Because of this, there is nothing to provide a context from which a coherent townscape might emerge. The more explicit and geometric the composition of the buildings, the less a design will permit anything that is non-geometric or vague. As a result the space loses all trace of human feeling. For all the soaring beauty of the individual buildings in the capital complex, they communicate a feeling of unutterable helplessness. With the buildings designed as geometric expressions of form, one cannot help thinking that they are not so much buildings for people—not even machines to live in—as sculptures to look at.

In this sense Chandigarh demonstrates that Le Corbusier was much more a designer, sculptor, and thinker than an architect. He was, nonetheless, a sculptor who thought in proportions to which we are not accustomed. Several hundred years from now, if any buildings constructed today are still standing, they will be only those of Le Corbusier. People of future centuries will visit these immense concrete monoliths as they would go to view the Acropolis. The D/H ratio for the large distance between buildings is higher than 3, so the entire complex can be viewed at one glance. The fact that Le Corbusier took the trouble to check his design by personally marking out the sites suggests that he had a sense for the sculptural quality of architecture, a quality that ensures the survival of his buildings for centuries.

Chandigarh is by no means the only example of new cities built on the kinds of principles Le Corbusier conceived. In Japan there is an extreme example in Tsukuba Academic Town, which is built around a newly established national university and a number of research institutes in the countryside near Tokyo. There are many others around the world. In some respects these cities make improvements over traditional plans, but in most something vital is lacking in the conception of a truly human townscape. For a clear judgment of the merits or faults of these cities, however, history will be our most eloquent critic.

The best examples in European masonry architecture of linear townscapes are found in Italian cities. As Bernard Rudofsky and Christian Norberg-Schulz have observed, in Italy a street can hardly be called a street without buildings crowded together closely on both sides. Indeed, in order for a street to become a townscape, a continuous row of buildings along it is an important prerequisite.

The linear streets of the past were limited to a distance that could be comfortably covered by walking, and they were really quite satisfactory, if only the problem of traffic could be solved. They made everything available within a reasonable distance and imparted a sense of continuity and unity for the people of a town. Today, pressed by the need to conserve energy in the wake of the recent oil crises, we would do well to take a new look at the linear pattern townscape. Of course, the traditional street can become clogged with vehicles, but we must identify and utilize the most desirable aspects of successful linear townscapes and incorporate them into our plans for modern cities.

Japan offers one type of example in its busy shopping and entertainment streets, which, as I observed earlier, are narrow, crowded, colorful, and lively, filled with intense human activity that is typical of the Asiatic townscape. In most cases the streets are 20 to 25 meters wide, which corresponds to the modular unit of approximately 70 to 80 feet.[8] If any wider, the structures on both sides of the street become isolated, and the enclosing effect of the buildings on both sides is reduced, sacrificing their Asiatic feeling. A D/H ratio of 1 is well balanced, and that of less than 0.6 gives a street a sense of intimacy and crowdedness, while one of 1.6 feels spacious and promotes a feeling of isolation. One of the most decisive components of the Asiatic street is the W/D ratio. When a relatively narrow street is fronted by buildings with wide facades, its overall atmosphere suffers. A survey of Japan's most lively streets shows that most have a W/D of 0.6 to 0.7. This results when shop fronts lining a street 8 meters wide are between 4.8 and 5.6 meters wide on both sides of the street, creating a distinctive atmosphere of thronged, lively activity typical of Asian cities. When the W/D ratio is higher, the townscape is diluted, and the feeling of homey, everyday bustle fades. The street with a low W/D gives the exterior space of the street an interior quality, especially, if in addition a roof is added over the street.

Here let us look at three popular, exemplary streets in the city of Yokohama—Motomachi, Chinatown, and Yokohamabashi Streets—in terms of their D/H and W/D ratios. Motomachi is a narrow street but, as one might expect in a port town, heavily influenced by western culture; it is stylish, and the goods for sale there are primarily imported, trendy western items. The street is 8 meters wide and extends 600 meters in length, with most of the 130 shops lining each side between 5 and 6 meters in width. The W/D is within 0.6 to 07, and many of the signboards and advertisements are written in roman letters (figures 112, 113a, and 114a).

Yokohama's Chinatown differs a little from its counterparts in New York or San Francisco because of its genuine Asiatic bustle. The street is 8.5 meters wide and 350 meters long. About 80 shops are lined up along each side of the street with a D/H of approximately 1. Most shops are about 5 meters wide, giving it a D/W of around 0.6. Red, yellow, and green colors abound, augmenting the festive, cluttered character (figures 115, 113b, and 114b).

Yokohamabashi Street is a typical example of the shopping street used by ordinary townspeople, and it is packed with shops and thronged with people. The street is only 7 meters wide and 350 meters long ($D/H = 1$) and has been made into an arcade by addition of a roof. About 140 shops squeeze together along the promenade, most between 2.7 and 3.6 meters wide, giving it a W/D of 0.4 to 0.5, the lowest of the three examples. The street is reserved for pedestrians, so automobile traffic is closed off. Partly because of the arcade roof, the street has the atmosphere of interior space, with the intimate qualities of the typical Asiatic establishments. Yokohamabashi is a favorite spot where local working people go to drink with their friends, to play *pachinko* ("vertical pinball"), or do their shopping (figures 116, 113c, and 114c).

As these examples of prominent shopping streets show, a natural length seems to fall between 300 and 600 meters. If much longer, they begin to lose their sense of coherence and unity. Most are between 7 and 12 meters wide with a D/H of about 0.6 to 1 and a W/D of about 0.6. Some unifying quality or principle gives the street its distinctive character, and those reserved for pedestrians are particularly cohesive.

112
Motomachi Street in
Yokohama
(Photograph: Sumiho
Ōta)

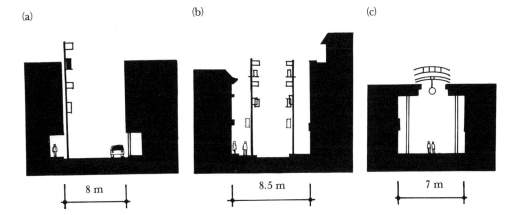

(a) (b) (c)

8 m 8.5 m 7 m

113
Sections of Motomachi
Street (a), Chinatown (b),
and Yokohamabashi
Street (c) in Yokohama

(a)

(b)

(c)

114
Plans of Motomachi
Street (a), Chinatown (b),
and Yokohamabashi
Street (c)

115
Chinatown, Yokohama
(Photograph: Sumiho
Ōta)

116
Yokohamabashi Street in
Yokohama
(Photograph: Sumiho
Ōta)

The streets described above all follow a single, straight-line pattern. My next example is of interest for its orientation to nodes in the townscape. Figure 117 shows three types of node-oriented streets, each with a distinctive character all its own. The typical Italian square is given in part (a); part (b) diagrams the Galleria of Milan, with its two nodes at either end where squares open on the La Scala theater and the Duomo. The configuration mapped in diagram (c) is that of the central section of Tokyo's Asakusa quarter, showing the shop-lined passageway leading up to Sensōji temple. These shops within the temple precincts, known as *nakamise*, have a history that goes back to the middle of the Edo period (1603–1868). The temple approach, about 25 meters wide and about 296 meters long, has changed little from the time it was built. Passing through the great main gate, flanked by guardian statues of the Deva kings, and beneath the giant paper lantern suspended inside, one can see the temple at the end of the two rows of shops lining the passageway (figure 118, parts a–e). While most of Tokyo is thoroughly internationalized, this street preserves the flavor of the Edo period, and the traditional atmosphere of this time is recreated by the enterprising, fun-loving, as well as pious, townspeople. The combination of the temple and these old *nakamise* makes the street especially dear to Tokyo citizens to this day. The position of the temple as the focus of the space at the head of the shops is particularly effective in enhancing Gestalt qualities.

Streets originally built for pedestrians have in modern times been almost completely taken over by automotive traffic. The shopping street reserved for pedestrians which has become a common feature of cities all over Japan is a measure

in defense against this trend. The first version of this kind of street was the so-called "pedestrian heaven" where traffic was blocked off on Sundays only, leaving the street open for strolling. This has been successful especially in the busy shopping quarters of Ginza, Shibuya, and Shinjuku in Tokyo.

The American trend toward turning existing streets into permanent pedestrian malls, is now beginning to take effect in Japan. The first of these was the shopping mall adjoining Hokkaido's Asahikawa station. This pedestrian mall is 20 meters wide and 1,000 meters long, and the space is punctuated with outdoor sculpture, water fountains, benches, and street lamps. The mall was not built without great difficulty, however, and was completed in 1972 only after overcoming numerous legal as well as economic complications through discussion between the mayor and local citizens. What draws our attention, in fact, is not so much the completion of this mall as the process of dialogue through which it was achieved. Later, many more of these malls were built, in Sakata, Sendai, and other cities, but perhaps the most successful example is the Isezaki mall in Yokohama (figures 119 and 120). This mall is 15 meters wide and follows a single line, 380 meters long. The street is attractively paved in patterned tile, and considerable care was given to the design of street lamps, telephone booths, clocks, benches, and other street furniture. This street was largely built through the cooperation between city officials and local citizens.

The numerous new conceptions of architecture we have seen challenge the theories that prevailed in the early part of the twentieth century; a new era of searching, experimenting, and testing has begun. The Metabolist, Mannerist, and

117
Three types of node-
oriented streets

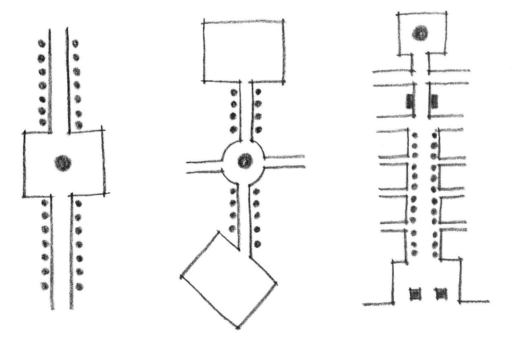

118
Passageway to Sensōji
temple in the Asakusa
quarter of Tokyo
(Photographs: Sumiho
Ōta)

(a)
Main gate from street

(b)
Close-up of gate and
lantern

(c)
Under main gate facing
shops

(d)
Shopping arcade
(*nakamise*); temple in
distance

(e)
Sensōji temple

119
Isezaki Mall in
Yokohama
(Photograph: Sumiho
Ōta)

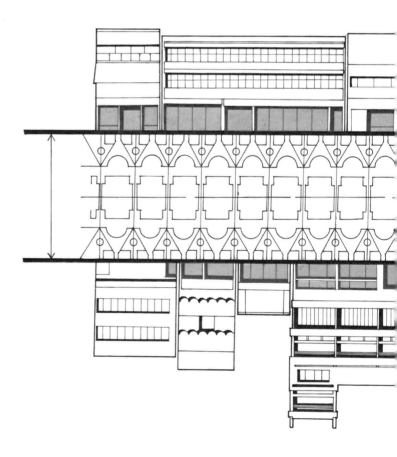

120
Plan and elevation of
Isezaki Mall in
Yokohama

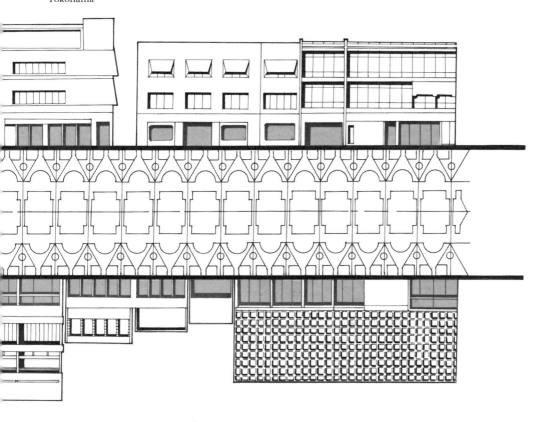

Postmodernist Movements and the applications of semantics and semiology to architecture have introduced a great variety of concepts and forms. These new approaches have had profound influence, but they will not necessarily determine the directions of architecture and the townscape. Ultimately products of local culture, the townscape must be comfortable and satisfying to the greatest number of inhabitants and meaningful in the context of a familiar conceptual framework. They cannot, and should not, be alienating to man.

I have given special attention to the works of Le Corbusier because I find that, notwithstanding his great achievements as an architect, his buildings were wanting in human qualities. His works represent an extremely refined sense of beauty based on formal aesthetics, but I cannot help the unsettling feeling that they implicitly overlook the existence of man himself. What I have hoped to do in this book is to show that townscapes must be predicated above all on the presence of human beings and to provide a practical guide to urban landscapes that affirm and celebrate the existence of man.

Notes

Chapter 1

1. Marcel Aymé, "The Walker-through-Walls," from *Across Paris and Other Stories*, trans. by Norman Denny (New York: Harper and Brothers, 1958), pp. 167–178.

2. "Sanjū-hachi-okunin: sumika—kabe no atsusa," [3.8 Billion People: Their Dwellings and Wall Thickness], *Asahi Shimbun*, June 9, 1974.

3. Otto F. Bollnow, *Neue Geborgenheit; das Problem einer Uberwindung des Existentialismus* [A New Sense of Security: The Existential Approach to the Problem of Conquest] (Stuttgart: W. Kohlhammer, 1960), p. 165.

4. Ibid., p. 167.

5. Gaston Bachelard, *The Poetics of Space*, trans. by Maria Jolas (New York: Orion Press, 1964), pp. 44–45.

6. Yoshida Kenkō, *Tsurezuregusa*, from a translation by Donald Keene in *Anthology of Japanese Literature* (Tokyo: Charles E. Tuttle, 1955), p. 233.

7. See *Satori no bunseki* [An Analysis of *Satori*] (Asahi Shuppansha, 1980).

8. Tetsurō Watsuji, *Fūdo: Ningengakuteki kōsatsu* (Iwanami Shoten, 1978), p. 144.

9. Ibid., p. 146.

10. See Yoshinobu Ashihara, *Exterior Design in Architecture* (New York: Van Nostrand Reinhold, 1970), p. 42.

11. Shinzō Kinouchi, *Toshi chirigaku kenkyū* [A Study in the Geography of Cities] (Tokyo: Kokin Shobō, 1951).

12. Watsuji, *Fūdo*, p. 49.

13. Lewis Mumford, *The Culture of Cities* (New York: Harcourt Brace Jovanovich, 1970), p. 54.

Chapter 2

1. Bernard Rudofsky, *Streets for People: A Primer for Americans* (New York: Doubleday, 1969), pp. 74–75.

2. Ibid., p. 19.

3. Jane Jacobs, *The Death and Life of Great American Cities* (New York: Random House, 1961), p. 29.

4. Noboru Shimamura et al., *Kyō no machiya* [Townhouses of Kyoto] (Kajima Shuppan: SD Sensho, 1971).

5. Rudofsky, p. 163.

6. Yoshinobu Ashihara, *Exterior Design in Architecture* (New York: Van Nostrand Reinhold, 1970).

7. Sekiyo Shimoide, *Dōkyō to Nihonjin* [Taoism and the Japanese] (Tokyo: Kodansha, 1976), p. 16.

8. Rudofsky, pp. 20–21.

9. Paul Zucker, *Town and Square: From the Agora to the Village Green* (New York: Columbia University Press, 1959), pp. 112–113.

10. See Ashihara, *Exterior Design in Architecture*, for an in-depth discussion of this phenomenon.

11. Bernard P. Spring, "Evaluation: Rockefeller Center's Two Contrasting Generations of Space," *AIA Journal* (February 1978).

Chapter 3

1. See Yoshinobu Ashihara, *Exterior Design in Architecture* (New York: Van Nostrand Reinhold, 1970), p. 50.

2. Yoshirō Kikegawa, "Gairo kūkan no shikaku kōzō" [The Perceptual Structure of Street Space], unpublished thesis, Faculty of Engineering, University of Tokyo, 1978.

Chapter 4

1. Henry Dreyfuss, *The Measure of Man: Human Factors in Design* (New York: Whitney, 1960), chart D.

2. Hans Märtens, *Der optische Masstab oder die Theorie und Praxis des asthetischen Sehen in den bildenden Kunstein* (Berlin: Ernst Wasmuth, 1884).

3. Tadahiko Higuchi, "Keikan no kōzō ni kansuru kiso kenkyū," Ph.D. dissertation, University of Tokyo.

4. Yoshinobu Ashihara, *Exterior Design in Architecture* (New York: Van Nostrand Reinhold, 1970), p. 119.

5. Gaston Bachelard, *The Poetics of Space*, trans. by Maria Jolas (New York: Orion Press, 1964), p. 172.

6. Ibid., p. 150.

7. Gaston Bachelard, *La Terre de les reveries du repos* (Paris: J. Corti, 1949). Reference may be found in *On Poetic Imagination and Reverie: Selections from the Works of Gaston Bachelard*, trans. by Colette Gaudin (Indianapolis: Bobbs Merrill, 1971), p. 98.

8. Serge Chermayeff and Christopher Alexander, *Community and Privacy* (New York: Doubleday, 1963), pp. 71–72.

9. Constantine E. Michaelides, *Hydra: A Greek Island Town* (Chicago: University of Chicago Press, 1967), p. 60.

10. Kevin Lynch, *The Image of the City* (Cambridge, Mass.: The MIT Press, 1960), p. 9.

11. Alvin K. Lukashok and Kevin Lynch, "Some Childhood Memories of the City," *American Institute of Planners Journal* (Summer 1956), pp. 142–152.

12. Kevin Lynch and Malcom Rivkin, "A Walk around the Block," *Landscape* (Spring 1959), pp. 24–34.

13. Gaston Bachelard, *La Terre*, p. 98.

14. Takeo Okuno, *Bungaku ni okeru genfūkei* [The Primal Setting in Japanese Literature] (Tokyo: Shūeisha, 1972), p. 29.

15. Ibid. *Menko* is a game played with pasteboard cards. In a common version a challenger attempts to flip an opponent's card lying flat on the ground by the sheer force of throwing another card near it, thus winning the challenged card.

16. Ibid., p. 17.

Chapter 5

1. Noboru Shimamura et al., *Kyō no machiya* [Townhouses of Kyoto] (Tokyo: Kajima Shuppankai, 1971).

2. See Edward Allen, *Stone Shelters* (Cambridge, Mass.: The MIT Press, 1969). In this square I made the acquaintance of Nicola Greco, and we instantly became friends. Greatly impressed by Cisternino's unique townscape, I inquired whether I might obtain survey maps and historical records of the city. The barber informed me that a study had already been done by American architect Edward Allen, who had spent two years in Apulia surveying the region and published the results in *Stone Shelters*.

3. Constantine E. Michaelides, *Hydra, A Greek Island: Its Growth and Form* (Chicago: University of Chicago Press, 1961).

4. Kōji Yagi, "Chūkinto no kikō to jūkankyō" [Climate and Living Environment in the Middle East], *Kenchiku zasshi* (June 1977), p. 27.

5. Nader Ardalan and Laleh Bakhtiar, *The Sense of Unity: The Sufi Tradition in Persian Architecture* (Chicago: University of Chicago Press, 1973), p. 99.

6. *The Architectural Review*, Iran Issue, vol. 159 (May 1976), p. 28.

7. Camillo Sitte, *City Planning According to Artistic Principles*, trans. by George R. and Christiane G. Collins (New York: Random House, 1965).

8. See my discussion in Yoshinobu Ashihara, *Exterior Design in Architecture* (New York: Van Nostrand Reinhold, 1970), p. 47.

Bibliography

General

Bachelard, Gaston, *La Poetique de l'éspace*. Paris: Presses Universitaries de France, 1957.

Bachelard, Gaston. *La Terre et les reveries du repos*. Paris: J. Corti, 1948.

Blake, Peter. *Form Follows Fiasco*. Boston: Little, Brown, 1974.

Bollnow, Otto Friedrich, *Neue Geborgenheit: Das Problem einer Uberwindung des Existentialismus*. Stuttgart: W. Kohlhammer, 1960.

Bollnow, Otto Friedrich. *Mensch und Raum*. Stuttgart: W. Kohlhammer, 1963.

Davey, Norman. *A History of Building Materials*. London: J. M. Dent & Sons Ltd., 1961.

Fortune Editorial Staff. *The Exploding Metropolis*. New York: Doubleday, 1958.

Frey, Dagobert. *Glundlegung zu einer vergleichenden Kunstwissenschaft*. Innsbruck/Vienna: Margarete Freidrich Rohrer, 1949.

Moholy-Nagy, Sibyl. *Native Genius in Anonymous Architecture in North America*. New York: Schocken Books, 1976.

Mumford, Lewis. *The Culture of Cities*. New York: Harcourt Brace Jovanovich, 1938.

Okuno, Takeo. *Bungaku ni okeru genfūkei—harappa, dōkutsu no gensō* [Primary Settings in Literature: The Fantasies of Fields and Caves] Tokyo: Shūeisha, 1972.

Ragon, Michael. *Les Erreurs Monumentales*. France: Librarie Hachette, 1971.

Saint-Exupéry, Antoine de. *Citadelle*. Paris: Éditions Gallimard, 1948.

Suzuki, Hideo. *Fūdo no kōzō* [The Structure of Climate and Culture]. Tokyo: Daimyōdō, 1975.

Ueda, Atsushi. *Nihonjin to sumai* [Japanese and Their Homes]. Tokyo: Iwanami Shoten, 1974.

Watsuji, Tetsurō. *Fūdo: Ningengakuteki kōsatsu* [Climate and Culture: A Study in Humanity]. Tokyo: Iwanami Shoten, 1935.

Lukashok, Alvin K., and Lynch, Kevin. "Some Childhood Memories of the City," *American Institute of Planners Journal* (Summer 1956), pp. 142–152.

Lynch, Kevin, and Rivkin, Malcolm. "A Walk Around the Block," *Landscape* (Spring 1959).

Lynch, Kevin. *Image of the City*. Cambridge, Mass.: The MIT Press, 1960.

Lynch, Kevin. *Site Planning*. Cambridge, Mass. The MIT Press, 1962.

Michaelides, Constantine E. *Hydra: A Greek Island Town*. Chicago: University of Chicago Press, 1967.

Nairin, Ian. *Counter-attack against Subtopia*. London: The Architectural Press, 1956.

Nairin, Ian. *Outrage*. London: The Architectural Press, 1955.

Norberg-Schulz, Christian. *Intentions in Architecture*. London: Allen & Unwin Ltd., 1963.

Norberg-Schulz, Christian. *Existence, Space and Architecture*. London: Studio Vista Ltd., 1971.

Rasmussen, Steen Eiler. *Experiencing Architecture*. Cambridge, Mass.: The MIT Press, 1959.

Rasmussen, Steen Eiler. *Towns and Buildings: Described in Drawings and Words*. Liverpool: The University Press of Liverpool, 1951.

Sitte, Camillo. *Der Stadtebau nach seinen kunstlerischen Grundsatzen* (first edition, 1889).

Sitte, Camillo. *The Art of Building Cities*. Trans. by Charles T. Stewart. New York: Reinhold, 1945.

Sitte, Camillo. *City Planning According to Artistic Principles*. Trans. by George R. Collins and Christiane Grasemann Collins, New York: Random House, 1965.

Thiel, Philip. "The Anatomy of Space," Unpublished manuscript, 1959.

Thiel, Philip. "The Urban Spaces at Broadway and Mason, A Visual Survey, Analysis and Representation," Department of Architecture, University of California, Berkeley, 1959.

Thiel, Philip. *Visual Awareness and Design*. Seattle: University of Washington Press, 1981.

Visual Structure

Arnheim, Rudolf. *Art and Visual Perception*. Berkeley: The University of California Press, 1954.

Dreyfuss, Henry. *The Measure of Man*. New York: Whitney Library of Design, 1959.

Gilbson, James J. *The Perception of the Visual World*. Boston: Houghton Mifflin, 1950.

Hall, Edward T. *The Silent Language*. New York: Doubleday, 1959.

Hall, Edward T. *The Hidden Dimension*. New York: Doubleday, 1966.

Metzger, Wolfgang. *Gesetze des Sehens*. Frankfurt: Waldemar Kramer, 1953.

Nelson, George. *How to See*. Boston: Little Brown, 1977.

Sommer, Robert. *Personal Space*. Englewood Cliffs, N.J.: Prentice-Hall, 1969.

Sommer, Robert. *Tight Spaces*. Englewood Cliffs, N.J.: Prentice-Hall, 1974.

Architectural and City Spaces

Allen, Edward. *Stone Shelters*. Cambridge, Mass.: The MIT Press, 1969.

Barnett, Jonathan. *Urban Design as Public Policy*. New York: McGraw-Hill, 1974.

Blumenfeld, Hans. "Scale in Civic Design," *Town Planning Review*, vol. 24 (April 1953), pp. 35–46.

Collins, George R., and Collins, Christiane Grasemann. *Camillo Sitte and the Birth of Modern City Planning*. New York: Random House, 1965.

Dijkema, Pieter. *Innen und Aussen*. Hilversum: G. Van Saane, 1960.

Gibberd, Frederic. *Town Design*. 3rd ed. London: Architectural Press, 1959.

Goldfinger, Myron, *Villages in the Sun*. London: Lund Humphries, 1969.

Hegemann, Werner, and Peets, Elbert. *The American Vitruvius: An Architect's Handbook of Civic Art*. New York: Architectural Publishing, 1922.

Jacobs, Jane. *The Death and Life of Great American Cities*. New York: Random House, 1961.

Jencks, Charles, and Baind, George, eds. *Meaning in Architecture*. London: Barrie and Jenkins, 1969.

Thiel, Philip. "A Notation for Architectural and Urban Space Sequences," Unpublished manuscript, 1960.

Thiel, Philip. "A Sequence Experience Notation for Architectural and Urban Space," *Town Planning Review*, vol. 32 (April 1961), pp. 33–52.

Thiel, Philip. "An Experiment in Space Notation," *Architectural Review*, vol. 131 (May 1962), pp. 320–329.

Paddington

Clarke, Albert N. *Historic Sydney and New South Wales*. Sydney: The Central Press Pty Ltd., 1968.

Freeland, J. M. *The Australian Pub*. Melbourne: Melbourne University Press, 1966.

Hiller, Rob. *Let's Buy a Terrace House*. Sydney: Ure Smith, 1968.

Roseth, John. "The Revival of an Old Residential Area," Ph.D. dissertation. University of Sydney, 1969.

Thompson, Patricia. *Paddington Sketchbook*. Sydney: Rigby Ltd., 1971.

Thompson, Patricia. *The Story of Paddington*. Sydney: The Fiveways Publishing Company, n.d.

The Paddington Society. *Paddington—A Plan for Preservation*. Sydney, 1970.

New York and Rockefeller Center

Balfour, Alan. *Rockefeller Center*. New York: McGraw-Hill, 1978.

Ballard, Robert F. R. *Directory of Manhattan Office Buildings*. New York: McGraw-Hill, 1978.

Manners, Marya. *The New York I Know*. Philadelphia: Lippincott, 1969.

Regional Plan Association. *Urban Design Manhattan*. London: Studio Vista, 1969.

Reid, W., Robbins, I. S., Madigan, F. V., and Carey, G. J. *Memo to Architects*. New York City Housing Authority, 1952.

Specter, David Kenneth. *Urban Spaces*. Greenwich, Conn.: New York Graphic Society, 1974.

Tauranac, John. *Essential New York: A Guide to the History and Architecture of Manhattan's Important Buildings, Parks, and Bridges*. New York: Holt, Rinehart and Winston, 1979.

White, Norval, and Willensky, Elliot. *AIA Guide to New York*. New York: Macmillan, 1967.

Italian Piazzas and Walled Cities

Boris, Franco, and Pampaloni, Geno. *Monumenti d'Italia: Le Piazze*. Novara: Istituto Geografico de Agostinin, 1975.

Cecchini, Giovanni. *San Gimignano*. Milan: Electa Editrice, 1962.

Croix, Horst de la. *Military Considerations in City Planning: Fortifications*. New York: Braziller, 1972.

Favole, Paolo. *Piazze d'Italia*. Milan: Bramante Editrice, 1972.

Imai, Toshiki. *Toshi hattatsu-shi kenkyū* [The History of Urban Development]. Tokyo: Tokyo Daigaku Shuppankai, 1951.

Italia Meravigliosa. *Piazze d'Italia*. Milan: Italian Touring Club, 1971.

Italia Meravigliosa. *Villa d'Italia*. Milan: Italian Touring Club, 1972.

Kiuchi, Shinzō. *Toshi chirigaku kenkyū* [A Study of Urban Geography]. Tokyo: Kokon Shobō, 1951.

Lotz, Wolfgang. *Studies in Italian Renaissance Architecture*. Cambridge, Mass.: The MIT Press, 1977.

Saalman, Howard. *Medieval Cities*. New York: Braziller, 1968.

Smith, Kidder G. E. *Italy Builds*. New York: Reinhold, 1954.

Todd, Malcolm. *The Walls of Rome*. London: Paul Elek, 1978.

Wolfe, Ivor de. *The Italian Townscape*. London: The Architectural Press, 1963.

Yamori, Kazuhiko. *Toshi puran no kenkyū* [City Plans]. Tokyo: Taimeido, 1970.

Zucker, Paul. *Town and Square*. New York: Columbia University Press, 1959.

Isfahan

Ardalan, Nader, and Bakhtiar, Laleh. *The Sense of Unity*, Chicago: The University of Chicago Press, 1973.

Eshragh, Abdol-Hamid (supervisor). *Masterpieces of Iranian Architecture*. Iran: The Ministry of Development, 1970.

"Iran Issue." *Architectural Review*, London, vol. 159, no. 951, May 1976.

"Iran: Yesterday, Today, and Tomorrow," *Art and Architecture*, no. 18–19 (June–November 1973).

Nihon Kenchiku Gakkai. "Chūtō no fūdo, kenchiku tokushū" [Climate and Culture of the Middle East: Special Issue on Architecture]. *Kenchiku zasshi*, vol. 92, no. 1123 (1977).

Rainer, Roland. *Anonymes Bauen in Iran*. Graz: Akademische Druck u. Verlagsanstalt, 1977.

Stierlin, Henri. *Iran of the Master Buildings*. Geneva: Editions d'Art Sigma, 1971.

Stierlin, Henri. *Isfahan-Image du Paradis*. Lausanne: La Bibliothéque des Arts, 1976.

Landscape

Appleton, Jay. *The Experience of Landscape.* New York: Wiley, 1975.

Campbell, Craig S. *Water in Landscape Architecture.* New York: Van Nostrand Reinhold, 1978.

Higuchi, Tadahiko. *Keikan no kōzō* [The Structure of Space]. Tokyo: Gihōdō, 1975.

Nakamura, Yoshio. *Doboku kūkan no zōkei* [The Formation of Engineered Space]. Tokyo: Gihōdō, 1967.

Simonds, John Ormsbee. *Landscape Architecture.* New York: McGraw-Hill, 1961.

Suzuki, Masamichi. "Fūdo, kenchiku, zōen no kōsei genri." [The Compositional Principles of Environment, Buildings and Gardens]. In *Randosukeipu dezain* [Landscape Design] Tokyo: Shōkokusha, 1978.

Townscape

Barley, M. W. *The House and Home: A Review of 900 Years of House Planning and Furnishing in Britain.* London: Studio Vista, 1963.

Deilmann, Harald, Bickenbach, Gerhard, and Pfeiffer, Herbert. *Housing Groups.* Stuttgart: Karl Kramer, 1977.

Hillairet, Jacques. *Dictionnaire historique des rues de Paris.* Paris: Les Editions de Minuit, 1964.

Hoffmann, Hubert. *Low Houses and Cluster Houses, An International Survey.* New York: Praeger, 1967.

La Brévine, Thomas. *Enchanted Paris.* Paris: Archaud, 1959.

Macintosh, Duncan. *The Modern Courtyard House.* London: Lund Humphries, 1973.

Nihon no machinami [Japan's Townscapes]. Tokyo: Mainichi Shinbunsha, 1975.

Nishizawa, Fumitaka *Kōto hausu ron* [A Study of Courtyard Houses]. Tokyo: Sagami Shobō, 1974.

Pennsylvania Avenue Development Corporation. *The Pennsylvania Avenue Plan.* 1974.

Rodofsky, Bernard. *Streets for People.* New York: Doubleday, 1969.

Sert, Jose Luis. *Ibiza.* Barcelona: Ediciones Poligrafa, 1967.

Sharp, Thomas. *Town and Townscape.* London: John Murray, Ltd., 1968.

Shimamura, Noboru; Shizuka, Yukio. *Kyō no machiya* [Townhouses of Kyoto]. Tokyo: Kajima Shuppankai, 1971.

Shimizu, Hajime. *Kyō no minka* [Houses of Kyoto]. Kyoto: Tankōsha, 1962.

Ueda, Atsushi, et al. *Machiya* [Townhouses]. Tokyo: Kajima Shuppankai, 1975.

Composition of External Space

Ashihara, Yoshinobu. *Exterior Design in Architecture.* New York: Van Nostrand Reinhold, 1970.

Ashihara, Yoshinobu. *Gaibu kūkan no kōsei/kenchiku yori toshi e* [The Composition of Exterior Space: From Building to City]. Tokyo: Shōkokusha, 1962.

Brambilla, Roberto, and Longo, Gianni. *For Pedestrians Only.* New York: Whitney Library of Design, 1977.

Carpenter, Edward K. *Urban Design Case Studies.* Washington, D.C.: RC Publications, 1977.

Chermayeff, Serge, and Alexander, Christopher. *Community and Privacy.* New York: Doubleday, 1963.

Costonis, John J. *Space Adrift.* Urbana: University of Illinois Press, 1974.

Design Council. *Street Furniture from Design Index.* London: Design Council, 1976.

Garland, Madge. *The Small Garden in the City.* London: The Architectural Press, 1973.

Goodman, Charles, and Eckardt, Wolf von. *Life for Dead Spaces.* New York: Fred L. Lavanburg Foundation/Harcourt, Brace and World, 1963.

Halprin, Lawrence. *Cities.* New York: Reinhold, 1963.

Halprin, Lawrence. *Freeways.* New York: Reinhold, 1966.

Halprin, Lawrence. *Notebooks 1959–1971.* Cambridge, Mass.: The MIT Press, 1972.

Halprin, Lawrence. *PROCESS: Architecture*, no. 4 (February 1978).

Kennedy, Declan, and Kennedy, Margrit. *The Inner City (Architects' Year Book XIV).* London: Paul Elek, 1974.

Malt, Harold Lewis. *Furnishing the City.* New York: McGraw-Hill, 1970.

Marlowe, Olwen C. *Outdoor Design: A Handbook for the Architect and Planner.* London: Crosby Lockwood Staples, 1977.

Pfannschmidt, Ernst-Erid. *Fountains and Springs.* London: George G. Harrap, 1968.

Seymour, Whitney North, Jr., ed. *Small Urban Spaces.* New York: New York Universtiy, 1969.

Spreiregen, Paul D. *The Architecture of Towns and Cities.* New York: McGraw-Hill, 1965.

Warren, Geoffrey. *Vanishing Street Furniture.* London: Newton Abbot, David and Charles, 1978.

Chandigarh and Brazilia

Boesiger, Willy, and Girberger, Hans. *Le Corbusier 1910–1965.* Zurich: Editions Girsberger, 1967.

Boesiger, Willy. *Le Corbusier 1952–1957.* Zurich, 1957.

Evenson, Norma. *Chandigarh.* Berkeley: University of California Press, 1966.

Jencks, Charles. *Le Corbusier and the Tragic View of Architecture.* London: Allen Lane, 1973.

Le Corbusier. *Le Modulor.* 1948.

Papadaki, Stamo. *Oscar Neimeyer.* New York: Braziller, 1960.

Staubli, Willy. *Brasilia.* Stuttgart: Verlagsanstalt Alexander Koch, 1965.

Index